Marathon
Running

Marathon
Running

From Beginner to Elite

Richard Nerurkar
Foreword by Steve Cram

A & C Black • London

For Bruce and Sue

Published in 2000 by A & C Black (Publishers) Ltd
37 Soho Square, London W10 3QZ.

Reprinted 2000; 2002

ISBN 0 7136 5351 5

A CIP catalogue record for this book is available from the British Library.

Acknowledgements
Cover photographs courtesy of Mark Shearman
Textual photographs courtesy of: Mark Shearman (pp. 2, 3, 5, 18 (bottom), 35, 36, 38, 44, 57, 58, 61, 67, 74, 79, 85 (bottom), 97, 106 (top and bottom), 108 (top), 120 (all), 126, 127, 129, 131, 137, 138); Ray O'Donaghue (pp. 8, 16, 29, 104, 108 (bottom); John Whetton (p. 133); the author (pp. 18 (top), 30, 85 (top), 98, 130, 139); and London Marathon (p. 91).
Line illustrations by Jean Ashley

Note: Whilst every effort has been made to ensure that the content of this book is as technically accurate and as sound as possible, neither the author nor the publishers can accept responsibility for any injury or loss sustained as a result of the use of this material.

Contents

Foreword

Steve Cram

As a sporting event the marathon is unique in many ways. In no other event could absolute beginners find themselves lining up alongside world champions and record holders with a common goal at a shared time and place. No matter what your standard, to conquer the 26.2 mile distance requires immense determination and a huge physical effort.

Richard Nerurkar had the supreme ability of making the whole thing look a lot less daunting. As Britain's most successful marathon runner during the '90s, he applied thought and practicality to his training, which took him amongst the world's elite. Winning the World Cup in San Sebastian in 1993 gave him the impetus to shoot for the World and Olympic titles. If all this book did was tell the story of Richard's personal challenges to reach the very top then that would be enthralling enough. But he has cleverly used his career landmarks to outline the building blocks for a successful marathon whether you are a first-timer or a seasoned campaigner. He intertwines his own marathon experiences with clear and practical information and advice on how to plan your training, diet, race tactics, recuperation and much more. Each chapter has the key points summarised making the book very easy to use.

Richard was a tough competitor and a meticulous planner. Here he has taken some of the hard work out of running the marathon for those who aim to follow in his steps. It will never be easy, as I now know, but this book should act as a guide for all marathoners – even for those of us who think we know a thing or two about running.

Morpeth, July 2000

Notes on terminology

Categories of runner

Beginner – starting running 'from scratch'
First-time marathon runner – perhaps a regular runner, but a newcomer to the marathon
Advanced – aiming to complete a marathon in under 3 hours
Elite – aiming to complete a marathon in under 2½ hours

Running distances – miles versus kilometres

Whereas in other European countries runners refer to distances in kilometres rather than miles, the reverse is more often the case in Britain. Yet even in Britain, certain set distances in kilometres – such as road races over 10 km – are familiar concepts to many runners.

Working in kilometres has a dual advantage: first, kilometres pass more quickly than miles and thus give you more reference points over the course of a long run; and second, in your training they allow you to mimic the system used at most major marathons, where drink stations are placed every 5 km along the route. Strength of tradition and habit will probably ensure, however, that you end up working in miles.

For the purposes of this book, accepted 'running parlance' has been used. Reference can be made, as useful or necessary, to the following conversions (equating to the common reference points during the course of a marathon):

1 km = 0.6 miles	21 km = 13.1 miles
5 km = 3.1 miles	25 km = 15.6 miles
10 km = 6.2 miles	30 km = 18.8 miles
15 km = 9.4 miles	42 km = 26.2 miles
20 km = 12.5 miles	

Types of training

Type of training	Definition
Repetitions ('reps')	Efforts of fast running over a short distance, followed by a period of recovery – the cycle being repeated a number of times
Fartlek	Literally 'speed-play'. A combination of fast and slow running, often based on a more flexible pattern of time/distance and effort/recovery
Tempo run	A single effort of sustained fast running
Pyramid	A session alternating easy jogging with brisk running – usually building up to a peak of either duration or intensity, and then declining again
Strides	Fast, but not flat-out sprinting over a short distance

Introduction

Taking up the challenge of the marathon

'You must be crazy – just thinking of it makes me tired.'
'I don't know how you do it – I can't even run to the end of the street!'
'What do you think of for all that time?'
'Don't you get a lot of injuries?'
'Do you do it for a living?'
'We'll be cheering you on in the Olympics.'
'Does that mean you're not allowed to eat chocolate?'

These are just some of people's reactions when I introduce myself as 'a marathon runner'. For some, the thought of running a marathon is not far short of their worst nightmare. For others, the reaction is rather one of amazement as they try to imagine what it must be like to cover – on foot and at speed – such a long distance. Still others are curious about how it is achieved. Some are filled with admiration; few are moved by envy; many simply want to encourage me on towards my goal.

Love it or hate it, people are fascinated by the marathon. When I tell them what I do, whether they react with curiosity or amazement, I know straight away that even without having run a marathon they have a sense of what's involved. People recognise that running a marathon involves a lot of effort and hard work. I may have a certain amount of talent to run well, but talent on its own doesn't count for very much unless I go out and do the training. That's true about anyone, at any level, wishing to run a marathon. To rise to the challenge of the marathon and complete the 26-mile distance involves a huge expenditure of effort and determination.

There is also a certain mystique about the event. Although you may have some idea of what's involved, until you've run your first marathon it's hard to appreciate the true nature of the marathon experience. It's one thing to observe the expressions of joy and relief of weary runners staggering exhausted over the finishing line, but it's quite another matter suffering those extremes of fatigue yourself as you fight your way to the end of the race. You might have a sense of how cruel the event can be from having seen runners collapse on the roadside, but without actually putting yourself through the same degree of exhaustion, how can you know what this feels like – or how in similar situations, other runners survive and drag themselves to the finish? Watching a marathon on television is worlds apart from experiencing it first-hand.

So what motivates people to run marathons? Let's face it, running is a simple activity. From early childhood it is one of our most natural activities. It requires effort, but not much technical expertise. As we leave our childhood behind, many of us grow out of the habit – which is why the thought of running even to the end

Dressed for the occasion: one of the many costumes seen
in London

of the street seems like hard work. The good news is, however, that with a little bit of training – or retraining – we can rediscover the ability to run. Of course, running in our adulthood involves more effort than it did when we were children, but once you have set yourself the goal of getting fit, the habit can be quickly relearned. For many, the next step up from wanting to get fit is deciding to run a marathon. It sounds crazy, I know, but it also speaks volumes for the special appeal of the 26-mile distance.

For running novices, the marathon offers a great challenge – accessible to and understood by many, but only accomplished by those brave enough to take the plunge. True, your training for the marathon will exhaust you and you might get to the finish of the race vowing never to run another one. But to have actually run a marathon represents a highly satisfying feat of willpower and endurance. Many runners decide to run a marathon having first watched countless others – slower, less athletic and more overweight than themselves – do precisely that in Britain's most famous and popular road race, the London Marathon.

Today, many people who are drawn into running marathons are also motivated by the desire to help other people by raising money and awareness for charity. 'If I'm going to put myself through the pain of running a marathon,' so their reasoning goes, 'at least I want to do it for a good cause.' Besides, why else would runners get dressed up as waiters, rhinos, toucans and superducks – and then attempt to run 26 miles?!

For regular runners, there may be a sense of not having completed one's running experience without having run a marathon. They feel they owe it to themselves to run one, not necessarily to achieve a certain time or position in a certain race, but rather to experience for themselves what the marathon is really like. The marathon is also a good yardstick by which they can assess (and profess) their running ability: to say that you are 'a 3½-hour marathon runner' sounds much more impressive than to profess to being 'a 75-minute 10-mile runner'. For many other regular runners, the marathon represents their one major goal for the year, and the result by which they compare their running fortunes from one year to the next.

'You may be in the same race as three or 30,000 others, but essentially the contest is between you and the distance.'

For elite athletes, the marathon may appeal for no better reason than that they are good at it. For sure, they enjoy the feeling of fitness and the process of training. But beyond this, there is the satisfaction of being able to perform at a level considerably above the capabilities of the ordinary person. These considerations outweigh the fact that a lot of effort and hard work, not to mention pain, is involved in the process of producing good results.

So, what's special about the marathon? First, everyone's a winner. The challenge is to cover 26 miles and 385 yards. You may be in the same race as three or 30,000 others, but essentially the contest is between you and the distance. For

'I've done it!' Elite athlete Joyce Chepchumba celebrates her victory and a new record in the 1999 London Marathon

most runners taking part in a big-city marathon, 'winning' means conquering the distance. It's also the only sporting competition where first-time marathon runners can 'toe the line' alongside Olympic champions. Even if you do not have a resting pulse of 32, weigh less than 60 kg, and run 120 miles a week, marathon running need not remain a passive interest. Whatever your background, the challenge is open to anyone prepared to commit themselves to the task of covering the distance.

As well as wondering what is so special about the marathon, people frequently ask, 'What do you get out of it?' Although this will obviously differ from person to person, most marathon runners will probably agree on the following:

- *It gives your life a focus.* To decide to run a marathon is like embarking on a mission. First-time marathon runners attempt to achieve a goal previously considered unimaginable. Many enjoy the sense of purpose gained from following a structured training programme. Experienced runners use the marathon as a pretext for adopting a more serious approach to their training at the start of their marathon build-up. As your marathon draws near, it's hard not to let the thought of the race, let alone your training and preparation, impinge on other areas of your life.
- *It's a shared experience.* Due to the growth in popularity of running over the past 20 years, the days of the lonely long-distance runner have become largely a thing of the past. Whatever standard of runner you are, training partners are at hand to accompany you on your weekend long run, or an evening session down at your local club. Even if you find yourself doing much of your running on your own in the build-up to a marathon, the thought of other runners working towards the same goal might spur you on in your training. You might also find that your non-running friends start to become interested in your marathon ambitions and share some of your excitement.
- *It's a personal achievement.* Most people who watch the London Marathon, while perhaps admiring the few gaunt-looking athletes at the front of the race, are more likely to identify with the thousands behind them whose only goal may be simply to get to the finish. These runners are not universally successful in achieving their time goal for the distance, nor do they always raise quite as much money for charity as they might first have hoped. Nevertheless, simply getting to the finish of the marathon represents a huge personal achievement.

However, while it's easy to romanticise the marathon experience – rising to challenges; fulfilling long-held ambitions; the exhilaration of performing at your best; enjoying a deep sense of satisfaction – the bottom line is that it is *tough*. It requires a great deal of hard training, sacrifices in terms of both time and energy, and lots of grit and determination to overcome those feelings of tiredness and pain. If you are thinking about running a marathon, think hard and carefully. It's a big commitment, yet if you stick to it I'm sure you won't be disappointed.

The aim of this book

A job done well always appears easy. This is certainly true of running marathons – except that the marathon has the potential for so many things to go wrong and wreck your plans. First you've got to survive the rigours of training without breaking down through illness or injury. Then, once you've got yourself to the start line, you have to negotiate your way round potential problems during the race. You might get a side-stitch at 10 miles or muscle cramp at the 20-mile point. At 15 miles you may find that you've drunk too much fluid, which is causing your stomach to churn around incessantly. You might be cruising along feeling fine with just six miles to the finish, only to find a few minutes later that you're on your knees as your last drops of energy drain away. You might end up running the last hour of the race suffering the agony of a blister every time your foot strikes the tarmac. Trying to eliminate these and other problems will increase your chances of success in the marathon. Helping you to do this is one of my motivations in writing this book.

I also wanted to write a book that went beyond a straightforward manual on marathon running. To do this I have tried to illustrate different aspects of marathon preparation and competition with reference to my own running experience. Over the past seven years of running marathons (and many more years before that as a committed distance runner), I have learned things from many people about training, race preparation and performance. This book gives me the opportunity to pass on what I have learned to others. Although in these more personal extracts my perspective is that of the elite competitor, my aim throughout has been to offer advice applicable to all levels of marathon runner, from the complete novice to the experienced competitor.

Mission accomplished – the finishing straight at London

In terms of structure, the book is divided into two sections. The first part, *What Every Runner Needs to Know*, starts out with the basics of designing a training routine and goes on to examine the key areas of training and preparation for running your marathon. In the book's second section, *Aiming For The Top*, the advice is more relevant for those who already have a fair amount of running experience – although I hope that other runners might be able to draw lessons even from these topics.

Each chapter contains a *Key points* section, which summarises the main learning points, followed by a *Useful tips* section of relevant, additional advice. I then give an insight into my own marathon experience, reflecting on the topic under discussion. Outlines of training schedules relating to various aspects of marathon training are given throughout the book; these are further supplemented in the Appendices, which contain complete training programmes for the marathon, from the five-hour runner to those at elite – or sub 2:30 – level.

My main hope is that this book will help you achieve *your* goals in running *your* marathon. By the time you finish reading, most of those earlier questions about marathon running should have been answered – though I leave it to you to guess whether or not I'm a chocolate-eating marathon runner!

Part 1

What every runner needs to know

Marathon coach Alan Storey (centre, in black) oversees a group of elite athletes

1 *Starting out*

The aim of this chapter is to introduce you to a routine of training. You're more likely to get fit by being consistent with a manageable amount of training, than by making heroic efforts which leave you worn out and dreading the arrival of your next workout. The secret is to be patient and enjoy seeing your fitness improve gradually over time.

Getting into the habit

Your first priority should be to start out gently and build up gradually. There's no need to think big yet. Learn to walk before you can jog; then combine some walking and jogging; then start to shift the balance towards doing more jogging than walking.

Try to find a regular time of day to exercise. Maybe you'll want to get it done first thing in the morning before the rest of the family is up and about, or perhaps fit it into your lunch-hour at work. Fixing a regular time in the day to exercise will make it easier for people around you. Soon they will expect to see you putting on your running shoes at a certain point in the day; this in turn should help you stick to your resolve.

Having a training partner can be a great stimulus to training in these early days – especially when the initial enthusiasm has worn off and the last thing you feel like doing is going out for a training run. Try to arrange at least one session per week with a friend or group of fellow runners.

You should give yourself at least six weeks both to get used to a training routine and to see improvements in fitness, and ideally you should have followed this routine for at least three months before you start a marathon-training programme. During this period, set yourself achievable goals; enjoy the novelty of going out to exercise; and keep reminding yourself of the progress you have made since you first started.

Before you get going, have a look at the *Useful tips* section on pp. 17–19. This offers some practical advice about how best to get started and stuck into a routine of training.

Structuring your training

If you're starting out as a running novice with a view to running a marathon, you will probably fall into one of two camps:

- the complete beginner, starting from scratch;
- the first-time marathoner – someone who has done a fair amount of exercise, perhaps including some running, but with little experience of having followed a structured programme of running training.

For both groups, it's good to get into the habit of making one of your weekly sessions last for at least an hour – for most people this will be easiest at the weekend – since this session will become a key part of your training once you start your marathon build-up.

The warm-up and warm-down

A training session, as distinct from simply taking exercise, can be thought of as a three-stage process involving preparation, performance and recovery. Your training begins by ensuring that you are appropriately dressed (*see Useful tips*, pp. 17–19) and warmed up (*see* below) – the 'preparation' phase. The 'performance' component of training involves walking or running for a set amount of time or distance. This is followed by a period of recovery which should ideally include both refreshment (taking in food and drink, perhaps having a shower) and relaxation (stretching and rest).

When you go out for a walk or easy run, your warm-up and warm-down may consist simply of a short sequence of easy stretching exercises (*see* pp. 156–160). When you progress to doing some faster running, I recommend that you begin by doing 5–10 minutes of easy running, followed by some stretching, before starting the main part of your workout. In this way you will be reducing the 'shock effect' upon your body, which in turn reduces the risk of getting injured. Then for the warm-down at the end of your hard effort, repeat the process of easy jogging and stretching.

The first two weeks

Here is what your first two weeks of training should look like:

The beginner

Table 1.1 Weeks 1 and 2 – the beginner

	Week 1		Week 2	
Session 1	Walk 30 min	Session 1		
Session 2	Walk 30 min	Session 2		Same as Week 1
Session 3	Walk 30 min	Session 3		
Session 4	Long walk or cycle – at least 1 hr	Session 4		

The first-time marathoner

Table 1.2 Weeks 1 and 2 – the first-time marathoner

Week 1		Week 2	
Session 1	Easy run 20 min	Session 1	Easy run 30 min
Session 2	Easy run 30 min	Session 2	10 min easy run for warm-up, then 1 min brisk followed by 1 min jog. Repeat 5 times, 5 min warm-down
Session 3	Easy run 20 min	Session 3	Easy run 30 min
Session 4	Run for 30 min or long walk/cycle at least 1½ hr	Session 4	Run for 40 min or long walk/cycle – at least 1½ hr

Brisk = a fast running pace but not sprinting
Easy = as slow as you like
Steady = faster than 'easy', but at a pace that still allows you to keep up a conversation with your training partner

Note: the timing doesn't have to be exact, but it may help to glance at a watch in order to keep the proportions about right. You may find (for the one minute of brisk running) that you prefer to count strides – roughly 90 'right-foot-downs' at a brisk pace will take one minute. Alternatively, if you find yourself running on a street with lampposts, you could jog for three lampposts, and then run briskly for four or five, rather than timing yourself.

The next two weeks

The beginner

Table 1.3 Weeks 3 and 4 – the beginner

Week 3		Week 4	
Session 1	Walk 30 min	Session 1	Walk 10 min; next 10 min, walk 1 min/ jog 1 min x 5; walk 10 min
Session 2	Walk 10 min; next 10 min, walk 1 min/ jog 1 min. Repeat 5 times; walk 10 min	Session 2	Walk 40 min
Session 3	Walk 30 min	Session 3	Walk 10 min; walk 90 sec/jog 90 sec x 2; walk 1 min/ jog 1 min x 4; walk 10 min
Session 4	Long walk or cycle – at least 1 hr	Session 4	Same as Session 4, Week 3

Note: if you find it pretty tough to jog for one full minute (*see* Week 3, Session 2), jog for about 100 m, then walk until you get your breath back again. An easier alternative to the walk/jog routine is easy walking/brisk walking.

The first-time marathoner

Table 1.4 Weeks 3 and 4 – the first-time marathoner

Week 3		Week 4	
Session 1	Easy run 30 min	Session 1	Easy run 30 min
Session 2	Run easy pace 15 min, then steady pace 15 min	Session 2	Warm-up 10 min easy running; then 2 min steady pace followed by 2 min jog. Repeat 4 times; warm-down 5 min
Session 3	Easy run 30 min	Session 3	Easy run 30 min
Session 4	Run 45 min or long walk/cycle for 1½ hr	Session 4	Same as Session 4, Week 3

The second month

The beginner

If you have built up gradually according to the schedules above, you should now feel confident to jog for two minutes at one stretch. Over the next few weeks you should aim to include as much jogging in your walk/jog sessions as possible without exhausting yourself. Keep in one walking-only session, and one longer session.

Table 1.5 The second month – the beginner

Weeks 5 and 7		Weeks 6 and 8	
Session 1	Walk/jog 30 min	Session 1	Walk 5 min/jog 5 min. Repeat 3 times
Session 2	Walk 5 min; next 20 min walk 2 min/ jog 2 min. Repeat 5 times; walk 5 min (in Week 7 try 2 min/ 3 min x 4)	Session 2	Jog 10 min, walk 5 min, jog 10 min (in Week 8 try a continuous jog for 20 min – go on, surprise yourself!)
Session 3	Walk 30–40 min	Session 3	Walk 30–40 min
Session 4	Long walk or cycle – at least 1 hr	Session 4	Long walk or cycle – at least 1 hr

The first-time marathoner

By the end of your first month of training, you will be doing at least two hours of running per week. Your aim over the next month is to increase gradually the total amount of running (up to three hours by the end of the second month) while introducing some faster running once or twice a week. Remember to respect the meaning of 'steady running' – it means making more of an effort than an easy jog, but still staying well below maximal effort.

Table 1.6 The second month – the first-time marathoner

Weeks 5 and 7		Weeks 6 and 8	
Session 1	Run easy pace 10 min, then steady pace 10 min x 2	Session 1	Steady run 30 min (40 min in Week 8)
Session 2	Easy run 30 min (40 min in Week 7)	Session 2	Easy run 40 min
Session 3	Warm-up 10 min easy run; then 1 min brisk (not flat-out)/ 1 min jog x 10; warm-down 5 min	Session 3	Warm-up 10 min easy run; then 4 min steady followed by 4 min jog, then 3/3, 2/2, 1/1; warm-down 5 min (add 5 min/ 5 min in Week 8)
Session 4	Run for 50 min (55 min in Week 7) or long walk/cycle for 2 hr	Session 4	Run 50 min (60 min in Week 8) or long walk/cycle for 2 hr

Entering your third month of training

You should be starting to feel much fitter now than when you started. As you continue to increase your training, listen carefully to any 'warning signs' from your body that you might be overdoing it. If you're particularly tired one day, don't be afraid to take a day off. You should also resist the temptation to time yourself over the same routes – vary the places and routes for your training runs (*see* also p. 45).

Here's your training plan for Weeks 9–12.

The beginner

Table 1.7 Weeks 9–12 – the beginner

Weeks 9–10		Weeks 11–12	
Session 1	Walk/jog 30 min	Session 1	Jog for 20–25 min (25–30 min in Week 12)
Session 2	Jog 10 min, walk 5 min, jog 10 min (in Week 10 continuous jog for 20 min)	Session 2	Jog for 20–25 min (25–30 min in Week 12)
Session 3	Walk/jog 30 min	Session 3	Jog/walk for 35 min, or continuous jog for 20 min
Session 4	Long walk/jog 45–50 min (try to jog as much as possible but don't be afraid to walk, especially up hills)	Session 4	Same as Session 4, Weeks 9–10

The first-time marathoner

Table 1.8 Weeks 9–12 – the first-time marathoner

Week 9		**Week 10**	
Session 1	Easy run 10 min, then 5 min brisk, 5 min easy, 5 min brisk; warm-down 10 min	Session 1	Easy run 10 min, then 6 x 2 min hard, 2 min jog recovery each time, easy 10 min
Session 2	Steady run 40 min	Session 2	Steady run 40 min
Session 3	1-1-2-2-3-3-4-4-3-3-2-2-1-1 min (alternating easy jog and brisk running, commonly known as a 'pyramid' session	Session 3	Warm-up 5 min; then 2 min steady/ 2 min easy x 6; warm-down 5 min
Session 4	Long run 60 min	Session 4	Long run 65 min
Week 11		**Week 12**	
Session 1	Easy run 10 min, tempo run 15 min, easy 10 min	Session 1	Warm-up 10 min, then 10 x 1 min running fast uphill with jog downhill recovery, warm-down 10 min
Session 2	Steady run 45 min	Session 2	Steady run 45 min
Session 3	30 min easy, then 8 x 100 m strides	Session 3	Warm-up 5 min; then pyramid: 1-1-2-2-3-3-4-4-3-3-2-2-1-1 min easy/steady; warm-down 5 min
Session 4	Long run 65 min	Session 4	Long run 70 min

Tempo = as fast as you can sustain for the given time/distance
Strides = running fast (feeling relaxed, not strained) over 100–120 m

Running for fun: participants in the Epsom Allsorts race run over 10 km

Running your first race

By the end of your third month of regular training, you should be ready to enter your first competition. The thought of racing might fill you with dread, but if you're thinking of running a marathon at some future date, you've got to start somewhere. Besides, running a race will give you some idea of how your training is going. A local 5 km or 10 km race is probably the best place to start. Don't be afraid of being left behind: you'll meet plenty of runners like yourself whose main ambition is not to run a fast time, but simply to get around.

If you plan to do a race at the end of Week 13, your final week of training before the race should look something like this.

The beginner

Table 1.9 Pre-race training – the beginner

Week 13	
Session 1	Jog 8 min/walk 2 min x 3
Session 2	Jog 20 min
Session 3	Have a rest day!
Session 4	5 km or 10 km race

The first-time marathoner

Table 1.10 Pre-race training – the first-time marathoner

Week 13	
Session 1	Warm-up 5 min, 5 min tempo/3 min jog x 3, warm-down 5 min
Session 2	Steady run 30 min
Session 3	Have a rest day!
Session 4	5 mile or 10 km race

If you have completed the programme above for your first three months of training, you will be in a much better position to embark on a marathon-training programme than when you first started out. You're now up and running, and ready to move on to the marathon build-up for real!

Key points

Consider carefully how best to fit exercise into your daily routine.
Don't be over-ambitious: set yourself achievable goals.
Aim for consistency in training, the key to improving fitness over time.
Vary your training routes, and if possible run on soft surfaces.
Don't always time yourself; go further not faster.
Be flexible and prepared to modify your training programme if need be.

Useful tips

Getting started

- *What do I wear?* Good supportive running shoes – not just your old pair of trainers that you used to play tennis in at school. Get a pair of shoes that are generous when your feet are at 'room temperature' as they will expand a bit as you run. Depending on the weather, you should exercise in a loose T-shirt and long tights or tracksuit bottoms (or shorts if you feel more comfortable in these). Women may want to buy a good sports bra from a department store or sports shop.
- *How fast should I run?* At a pace that is relaxed and comfortable. Initially this may be just a walk, but soon you should be able to combine this with a short jog (*see* training schedules, pp. 10–15). If you have a training partner, you should exercise at a pace which allows you to talk. Remember, in these early stages it's better to go further than faster.
- *Where should I run?* Preferably away from busy streets, but if you are running in the dark then it's better to stay on well-lit routes. Ideally you should do some of your running off-road, perhaps in a nearby park or along some dirt trails: your legs suffer less pounding on softer surfaces and your surroundings will make you feel more at ease. It's also good to vary your routes. If you

'There's no such thing as bad weather, only inappropriate clothing': training with Kenyan runners in Colorado in 1996

Off-road running is best for body and mind

always complete the same circuit, it's easy to get into the habit of racing yourself over the distance. You can do this once every two weeks perhaps, but not every day.

- *How can I reduce the risk of breakdown through illness or injury?* By warming up properly, stretching well (*see* pp. 156–160) and giving your body time to recover from strenuous bouts of exercise. Give your body a chance to warm up, too, by progressing either from a walk to a jog or (if you're fitter) from an easy jog to a run – it does little good, and may even cause you an injury, if you sprint off from the start. Stretching post-exercise, in particular for the calves, hamstrings and quadriceps, will help guard against acute feelings of stiffness. If you have time and opportunity, have a swim or sauna – ideal for tired muscles after a run. Rest should also be seen as an important component of training, so that you don't wear yourself out completely. Just because things appear to be going well, don't do too much too soon. Finally, use the training schedules sensibly and be prepared to modify them according to your lifestyle.

- *(For women) Can I run when I have my period?* Yes, running may even help ease the discomfort through the release of pain-relieving endorphins.

- *Should I change my diet?* Your running will benefit if you are eating a healthy, well-balanced diet: lots of fruit and vegetables, a good supply of carbohydrate-rich food and sufficient protein (*see* Chapter 4 for more detail). Fatty foods should be kept to a minimum. Make sure too that you keep adequately hydrated; for every 20 minutes of running you should drink about 300 ml of fluid, and drink more when training in hot conditions. Whatever time of day you exercise, it's good to take some food and drink soon after finishing. Eating and drinking sensibly will help you to recover more quickly from the exertions of training.

- *Where can I get more advice?* The monthly running magazines available on most news-stands are a good source of information about many training-related issues. They often contain advice on overcoming injury and improving your diet; updates on the latest shoe models and items of sportswear; and motivational stories about runners who once started out just as you are now doing.

Becoming a marathon runner

In April 1985, midway through my undergraduate course at Oxford University, I was selected to represent a combined Oxford-Cambridge athletics team on a tour to compete against the Ivy League colleges in the USA. On one of our rest days after a competition in Providence, Rhode Island, we were given the option of going to the beach in Newport or going to watch the Boston Marathon. For the distance runners on the team, it was an easy decision to make. This was one of the world's most famous marathons, with a history that went back to the start of the modern Olympics. It would also be my first opportunity to witness a marathon 'in the flesh'. Soon we were on the road, heading north up I-95 towards Boston.

My first marathon experience

By the time we parked the car at the 22-mile point at Cleveland Circle, word had reached us that the pre-race favourite, Geoff Smith from England, had gone off like a madman, passing through 10 km at world-record pace in 29:05. We ran over to a local bar on the corner of Cleveland Circle, where the television screen showed Smith going further and further away from the rest of the field. He was attacking Steve Jones' recent world-best mark of 2:08:05 for the marathon. Excitement grew as Smith reached 20 miles still on schedule to set a new world-best. Then suddenly, as we watched on the screen, disaster struck. He stopped and clasped his hamstrings. He walked a bit, then started jogging. He covered the 21st mile in over six minutes. By the time he came past us, he was doing all he could just to keep going. His earlier serious demeanour had turned to one of disbelief. At this point, Smith was still over a mile ahead of the second-placed runner. Somehow he managed to claw his way to the finish in a time of 2:14:05, six minutes outside Jones' record, but still with a winning margin of over five minutes. We left Boston that afternoon having learned how cruel and unforgiving an event the marathon can be.

Making progress

In my final year as a student, I finally made a breakthrough into big-time athletics by gaining selection to compete on the British team at the 1989 World Cross-Country Championships in Norway. Led home by Tim Hutchings, who won the individual silver, the British team finished second behind Kenya. I was 49th. And so, at the age of 25, my international career was underway. I was dubbed a late developer, though I had actually been running seriously for over 15 years. At the age of nine I had won a bag of crisps for breaking the record in the school race. Now I was gaining international honours.

In my years as a schoolboy and then student runner I had enjoyed some success, but I was still some way off being among the very best. Why had I kept at it for so long, if success alone had not been the sole motivating factor? I was still running because it was something I enjoyed. I enjoyed the fun of running with others. I enjoyed the feeling of wellbeing it gave me. I enjoyed, too, the challenges it provided. And I enjoyed the satisfaction of doing well and improving at it, even when I was not winning. By now, running had become part of my identity.

Stepping stones to my first marathon

Three years later, after a disappointing 17th place finish in the 10,000 m final in the 1992 Barcelona Olympics, I took an end-of-season break. At the beginning of October, I started to plan out my training for the winter leading up to my first marathon – scheduled for the following spring. It had long been my intention to move up from the 10,000 m to the marathon. I was now 29 years old, and thus at a stage of my development when I was both physically and mentally strong enough to master the distance. While I still had a number of years of my international career ahead of me, I wanted to start gaining experience at the marathon. If things went to plan, I hoped to reach my peak in time for the next Olympics in Atlanta.

My coach, Bruce Tulloh, was keen for me not to make any drastic changes to the training that had served me so well for the past few years. As a 10,000 m runner I was already running a high weekly mileage, so moving up to the marathon only required a slight shift of emphasis towards greater endurance, and this could be introduced gradually over the course of the winter. In fact, for most of the autumn I stuck with my familiar routine, which included lots of good aerobic running and a number of good 10 km workouts designed to improve my speed. The only slight changes were an increase in the duration of my long endurance run at the weekend, and the introduction of more regular interval workouts on the road, run over longer distances at a more controlled pace. Even though I wasn't yet into a marathon build-up for real, Bruce was already keen for me to start shifting my thinking towards the event.

The winter got off to a good start when I ran a personal best for the half-marathon of 1:01:33 in Orlando, Florida in early December. It looked as though I was well on target for a promising debut. But in February 1993 I picked up an illness that forced me to withdraw from the British team for the World Cross-Country Championships, the first time I had missed the event since 1989. The virus prevented me from resuming normal training until the last week of March, leaving me little time to prepare for my debut marathon, originally planned for the first weekend of May. From all the good training I had done since the previous summer I knew I had the background to run a good marathon; but at the same time I realised there was no need to rush my marathon build-up. In view of this, I decided to postpone the date of my debut marathon by three weeks, and set myself the task of preparing for the Hamburg Marathon on 23rd May 1993.

A low-key approach

I went into my first marathon deliberately trying not to put any pressure on myself. The fact that I had only recently recovered from my illness – thus curtailing the length of my build-up – also helped to ensure that I had modest ambitions this time around.

My aim was to get a feel for the distance – not to break any records. I wanted to come out of the race with a positive first experience. If I was serious about embarking on a career as a marathon runner, it made more sense to be cautious than over-ambitious. It would certainly do my confidence no good to blow up disastrously, or even worse, fail to finish at my first attempt.

My plan was to run at an even pace for the entire distance. I then had to determine what time I should aim for at the halfway point. The previous autumn I had run 1:01:33 for the half-marathon; and three weeks before my debut in Hamburg, I had run 1:02:39 on an undulating course in Exeter. On this basis I reckoned that I should be able to reach halfway in the marathon in around 66 minutes without feeling too tired, and then aim to finish in around 2:12.

Pre-race arrangements

I flew out to Hamburg two days before the race. I knew the city well from my student days, when I had worked in Europe as a bus tour guide, so I was already able to picture parts of the marathon route from the course map which I had received before leaving home. Bruce, his wife Sue and my mother – my three most stalwart supporters throughout my athletic career – flew out with me, and we were soon checked into our hotel, situated less than a five-minute jog from the start and finish of the course in the centre of Hamburg.

On the day before the race there were a few matters to attend to. First, we were driven round the course by the race organisers. Then, there was a technical meeting at which all the final pre-race details – such as arrangements for the special drinks stations – were given out. The weather was predicted to be cool with a slight breeze.

In an attempt to beat the existing course record of 2:10:43, we were told that the intended pace of the leaders for the first half of the race would be 1:05:00. This meant that I would have to restrain myself from going off with the leaders, since I had deliberately set myself a more conservative halfway target of 1:06:00.

In the morning, and again in the early evening, I did an easy 20-minute run which took in the last 2 km of the course – on the basis that it's far more important to know how the race finishes than how it starts. The remainder of my pre-race day was spent relaxing with my feet up in my hotel bedroom, while my supporters familiarised themselves with the transport system that they would be using the following day to get round the course.

My debut in Hamburg had received relatively little pre-race coverage in the athletics media, which helped to take the pressure off me. David Powell, athletics correspondent for *The Times*, was the only journalist who had travelled out to Hamburg to report on the race. On the evening before the race we met up with him in the hotel, and the five of us went out for a pasta meal together.

Race-day in Hamburg

An hour before the race began on race-day morning, I walked the short distance to the start with Bruce. My legs were feeling loose even before starting my warm-up, so I held myself back from doing too much running prior to the start of the race. I jogged easily for five minutes, did some stretching, jogged for another five minutes, and did a few strides. Just before 9.00 a.m. we were called to the elite start, and the race got underway.

My main point of focus in the early few miles was not to run too fast; I had no intention of charging off at the pace of the leaders. Glancing at my watch after the first kilometre, I realised that I had run slower than intended (3:14 min/km as opposed to my target pace of 3:07), so slightly raised my tempo for the next few miles. At the first drinks station after 5 km, race officials were trying to help the runners by handing them their special drinks. However, they had failed to pick up my bottle, so I virtually had to stop and push my way through to find it. At this stage of the race, refuelling was more important than a few seconds lost. From then on, I gradually worked to get back on to my pre-race schedule, passing the 10 km point in 31:12. The leaders were by now out of sight, and I was running on my own.

I kept reminding myself to stay relaxed and conserve my effort for later in the race. Soon after the 15 km drinks station I started to get a stitch, possibly from having drunk too much fluid at the first three stations, so I decided not to take my bottle at the next station. At 20 km I quickly started to gain on a group of runners whom I then passed at the halfway stage (1:05:53).

Unbeknown to me, the leaders were over a minute up on me at this point, having run 1:04:40 for the first half of the race. At 25 km I still felt relaxed, though I was now running faster than at the start of the race. The Belorussian Vladimir Kotov, ran behind me for a couple of kilometres, but by 28 km I was again running on my own. Bruce called out to me that I was in fifth place, about 30 seconds down on the leaders. At 30 km the lead car came into view. Soon I passed the fourth-placed runner, and within a further 2 km I had caught up the two race leaders. With six miles of the race to go, I stopped thinking about pace and started thinking about how I might win the race.

For the next 5 km I ran a few strides behind the two race leaders. Though we were still running quite fast (3:06 min/km), it felt much easier because I was now following rather than setting the pace. I gathered my strength to make a decisive attack. At the 23-mile point I surged ahead of the two African runners, and from then on continued to extend my lead. I came into the finish 41 seconds clear of the second-placed runner, Thomas Naali of Tanzania. My winning time was 2:10:57. I had run the second half of the race in 1:05:04, almost 50 seconds faster than the first half.

This had been a great start to my marathon career. In terms of my finishing time, I had comfortably achieved my goal, and done this by running faster over the second half of the course than over the first. My time was only seven seconds slower than Eamonn Martin's winning time in London a month previously. Winning the race had been a bonus.

Postscript

Six hours after breasting the tape to complete my first marathon, I found myself staggering through the concourse at Hamburg airport. It had been a long day since our pre-race breakfast at 5.50 a.m. Satisfaction with my performance, coupled with relief that the task had been accomplished, could not disguise an acute feeling of post-race weariness. My feet were still hot from pounding over 26 miles of tarmac. I had one or two nasty blisters. Bruce helped me by carrying my trophy, Sue held the bouquet of flowers. We had to return to London that evening, because on the following morning I was due to fly off to St. Petersburg in connection with some work I was doing for a church agency – and my flight to Russia was leaving at 6.55 a.m. If it was true that I had played down my ambitions before the race, it was also the case that I had underestimated quite how tired I would be feeling afterwards.

My induction into the world of marathon racing had been a successful one. After many years of watching the event, I had at last experienced one for myself. Admittedly, the goals for my first marathon had been relatively modest; though after the uncertainties caused by my virus this seemed only right for my first attempt at the distance. Bruce and I felt there was much more to come and we had already started to map out the route ahead. We both felt excited about my future career as a marathon runner.

2 The marathon build-up

How long do you need to prepare for a marathon? If you are starting from scratch, you should ideally give yourself at least a year of regular training before even thinking about running a marathon. During this period you can gradually extend the distance of your longer runs, as well as the total number of runs and miles that you are doing each week. Your first major goal towards the end of this period should be to run a half-marathon, and when you've achieved this you can then start to set your sights on running the full 26-mile distance.

The longer your preparatory period of developing fitness, the more confident you will feel when you come to think specifically about training for a marathon. The minimum length of preparation that I advocate for the first-time marathon runner is the three-month period outlined in Chapter 1. Thereafter the *build-up* itself – the period of marathon-specific training – should last a further three to four months. (Its exact length will depend on your running experience and your level of fitness.)

Table 2.1 is designed to help you – as a first-time marathoner – assess your readiness to embark on a three-month marathon build-up, relative to your goals. The key point here is not to stick rigidly to the figures shown, but to set your goals for your marathon according to the level of running that you have attained before starting your marathon build-up.

Table 2.1 Assessing your readiness for a three-month build-up as a first-time marathon runner

Marathon goals	Regular training before build-up	Volume of weekly running	Previous race experience
Complete the distance	3 months minimum	15 miles per week	5–10 km
< 4½ hr	3–6 months	25 miles per week	Half-marathon
< 4 hr	6–12 months	25–30 miles per week	Half-marathon in < 2 hr
< 3½ hr	12 months +	35 miles per week	10 km in < 44 min*; half-marathon in < 1 hr 40 min*

*These times may differ both between and among male and female runners, so are only an approximate guide. In general, female runners aspiring to these goals should be further under this upper limit than male runners.

More advanced runners may be interested to see how I determined the length of my marathon build-ups based on my fitness level immediately beforehand (*see* Table 2.2). Note how my build-up periods were sometimes shorter than three months, simply because I already had a good base of endurance from the preceding block of training. When the pre-marathon period included more racing and a reduction in the volume of training (as in the autumn of 1993), I used a full 12-week build-up.

Table 2.2 Determining the length of the marathon build-up

Pre-build-up phase	Level of fitness at start of build-up	Length of build-up	Event and date
10,000 m track race, followed by 3 weeks at altitude, 2 more track races, then one easy week	Good 5 km track speed but short of endurance	12 weeks	San Sebastian, October 1993
8 weeks of track training and racing, finishing with 10,000 m track race, then one easy week	Good base of endurance after 10 km training	10 weeks	Helsinki, August 1994
3 weeks at altitude, then one easy week followed by 2 cross-country races	Still enjoying benefits of good training at altitude	10 weeks	London, April 1997

Structuring a 12-week build-up

The great thing about running training is that you can often start to see returns on your hard efforts within quite a short space of time. Within a six-week period, many runners can notice substantial gains in fitness. However, the art of successful training is to make small, gradual increases in your training loads from one week to the next, rather than to let your enthusiasm get the better of you and build up too hastily. An over-hasty start can not only lead to you flagging halfway through the build-up; it may also lead to injury and breakdown. Better to plan your training so that your body hardly notices the slight increases in training as you start to get fitter and progress towards your goal.

One useful way of viewing the overall pattern of a marathon-training programme is to divide your 12-week build-up into four quarters of three weeks each. As you progress from one quarter to the next, you gradually increase the volume and intensity of your training, so that by the third quarter you should be training at your hardest. Think of the four phases of your build-up as 'training well' (first phase); 'training hard' (second phase); 'training very hard' (third phase); and 'easing down and preparing to compete' (fourth phase). The final quarter is when you gradually start to reduce the amount of training and prepare to perform at your best in the race itself. Table 2.3 provides an example of this graduated approach to training loads over the course of a marathon build-up.

Table 2.3 Graduated training during the build-up

Training unit	Level	1st quarter	2nd quarter	3rd quarter	4th quarter
Weekly long	Marathon novice	10–13	14–17	18–20	‹15
run (miles)	Advanced (‹3 hr)	13–16	17–20	21–24	‹18
Total weekly	Marathon novice	20–30	30–40	40–50	‹40
mileage	Advanced (‹3 hr)	50–60	60–70	70–80	‹60

The length of your weekly long run should increase by small increments during each phase of the build-up (here, a three-week period) as well as from one phase to the next (as Table 2.3 shows). For those running up to 40 miles per week, total weekly mileage should increase by not more than 20% from one week to the next; for those running more than 40 miles per week, the increase should be no more than 10% from one week to the next. The merit of planning out the overall structure of your training in this way is that you learn to retain your enthusiasm and determination to train hard for when it is most needed – a skill that will also serve you well when it comes to running the marathon itself.

Note how the hardest phase of the training takes place once you are into the second half of the build-up. Structuring your training in this way will improve your chances of staying healthy and free of injury. The human body has an amazing capacity to adapt to new stresses placed upon it, but to allow it to do this you must be sensible in introducing those new stresses gradually. Too much stress at any one time will lead to breakdown.

Stuart's story

Just before Christmas last year, Stuart was one of over 30,000 runners around the country who received a letter through the post telling them that their entry had been accepted to run in the London Marathon the following April. For the past two years Stuart's application through the lottery had been rejected, so he was overjoyed to get his acceptance letter this time around. Having started running just over two years ago, and having competed in a number of local 10 km road races, at last this was his chance to see how fast he could cover the 26-mile distance. With a lot of hard training and a bit of luck, he thought, maybe he could realise his ambition of running a marathon. He even set himself the challenge of breaking the four-hour barrier.

Since sending off his entry in October, Stuart hadn't held out high hopes of having his entry accepted. In fact, as the autumn progressed he had got out of his regular routine of training and felt that he was slowly losing fitness. When news of his acceptance came through, he resolved to get serious again about his running once the Christmas festivities were over.

January 1st came around and he started the New Year with a long run to his wife's parents that took him over 1½ hours, longer than any run he had done previously by almost 20 minutes. The following week he was out running regularly on the dark, icy roads around his home, and had planned a route for his long run the following weekend. Soon he was beginning to notice an improvement in his fitness, and in his new-found enthusiasm he decided to increase his training load by introducing a midweek sustained tempo run, first over six miles, and then the following week up to nine miles. In the last week of January he managed to run a total of 48 miles, his highest weekly mileage ever. If he continued at this rate, he figured, in a month's time he might be able to run a 60-mile week. Off that sort of training he might even be capable of running a 3½-hour marathon.

The only problem was that he was already starting to feel a little twinge in his left calf, a problem that seemed to get worse the longer and faster he ran. By now Stuart was running every evening of the week, in addition to a speed session on Saturday and his Sunday-morning long run. He had little time left over to spend with his wife and baby daughter, or his non-running friends, let alone to see a doctor about his injury despite it getting sorer as the weeks went by. Finally, after a painful 15-mile run one Sunday in the middle of February – which reduced him at the end to little more than a hobble – he decided to take a few days' rest and get his injury seen by a specialist. His physiotherapist advised him to take three weeks off running.

'Hasten slowly'

Stuart's story is not uncommon among aspiring London Marathon runners, especially those attempting the event for the first time. He had plenty of determination to do the necessary training. He was willing to make sacrifices to fit more hours of running into his lifestyle. He even knew the right components of marathon training. His fault lay rather in his haste to build up his fitness too quickly, since he failed to realise that he had plenty of time on his side. Stuart would have done better had he adopted a more graduated approach to his training. Gains in fitness on a week-by-week basis might have then appeared smaller, but he would have reduced the risk of injury and given himself more chance of success over the extended period of a full three-month marathon build-up.

Hard and easy training

Stuart's story illustrates the importance of building up fitness gradually, as well as allowing sufficient time to recover from hard efforts in training. One way of achieving this is to plan some 'easy' days (or even an easier week) of running into the cycle of your training – *before* your body forces you to do so. This also has the benefit of allowing you to fit your running around other commitments in your life. For instance, if you are able to anticipate a particularly busy week ahead at work, or a family weekend away that will prevent you from doing your usual training, use this period to reduce your training and give your body a chance to recover.

The duration of such easy periods depends on the length and intensity of the previous period of training. In general, the harder and longer you train, the greater the need for recovery. In order to minimise the risks of breakdown you should limit the duration of your heaviest period of training to between two and three weeks. At lower volumes and intensities of training, there is less need for easy periods of training, and it makes more sense to progress consistently over an extended period.

Whatever approach you take, you will undoubtedly benefit from having a plan and structure to your training. Use the training programmes on pp. 145–146 and 147–155 as a guide for setting a schedule that suits your habits and your routine. 'If you fail to plan, you plan to fail', goes the saying – so make sure you have a plan before you get stuck into the training.

Key points

Plan out a structure for your marathon build-up.
Assess your state of readiness at the start of your build-up, and adjust your goals accordingly.
Increase your training loads by small, gradual increments.
Divide your build-up into phases of progressively increased effort, with the hardest effort coming in the second half of the programme.
Stay on top of your training by scheduling easy days to follow particularly hard periods of training.

Useful tips

Coaching lessons

Sometimes, even good mountain climbers can benefit from the services of a guide. In this respect runners are no different – they too can often be helped through the advice of a coach, partner or friend. A good coach or adviser can act as the 'outside voice', understanding the desires and motivation of the athlete while still being detached from the physical and emotional stress of training. They are therefore better able to make more rational judgements when it comes to deciding on training. Coaching involves not merely the task of setting good training schedules; it also requires understanding of the athlete's particular needs.

Some of the important roles performed by the coach or adviser are:

- *Preventing you from becoming a slave to your training schedule.* As your individual circumstances change, it's important to be flexible with your training programme. Sometimes you may need to modify your training to make allowances for stresses in other areas of your life, or if you pick up a slight illness or injury. It's not always easy for the athlete alone to strike a balance between being disciplined about following a schedule and sensible about making such adjustments. A coach might be the person to help you.
- *Telling you when you've done enough.* The competitive nature of the athlete often means that he or she may want to do more training, when more will result only in an increased risk of injury or illness. A coach can help reassure you that enough good training has been done and that you will benefit more from stopping now, before you get too tired.
- *Offering encouragement when you're feeling down.* In the course of any training programme, there are bound to be times when things don't work out quite as you had planned. Maybe you pick up a small injury and have to take a few days off running; maybe you feel too exhausted to train, or simply lose motivation for a while. At such times, it's often good to be able to turn to

Family encouragement

someone who is able and willing to support you in your training. Maybe they're able to join you for a bike ride when you are forced to take a break from running; or share some of the stress from another area of your life; or simply cook you a good meal to perk you up again.

- *Giving you confidence.* While fitness is usually measured in terms of your ability to cover set distances in certain times, your readiness to perform well either in training or competition also depends on how confident you are about accomplishing the task ahead of you. A coach can help in this respect, by being both supportive *and* realistic.

Every runner's requirements are different. Some will be better at thinking for themselves and at applying the brakes on training when they become too tired. Others might respond well to having a friend watch them train or follow them in the car or on the bike. Others will never be short of motivation but need reassurance that their training is going to plan. At some stage in the course of training, most of us benefit from the support and advice of a good friend. Remember too that the best coach for you isn't necessarily the person with the most running expertise; it may be the person who knows you best and understands what you are trying to get out of your running.

Here's a brief account of how my coach Bruce played a crucial part in helping me get the most out of my running.

Long before we first met, I knew of Bruce's reputation as both a highly accomplished athlete and coach. As one of Britain's best distance runners in the 1960s, and known for his barefoot running, Bruce is perhaps best remembered for winning the 1962 European 5000 metres in Belgrade. After he retired from international competition, he set a world record in 1969 by running from Los Angeles to New York in 64 days. Since then, as well as writing numerous books on training, he has helped many athletes achieve success at school, national and international level.

At the time of our first meeting in 1986, towards the end of my student days at Oxford, Bruce was coaching – in addition to his three children – a close friend and rival of mine from the Cambridge University team. This was my first regular contact with an athletics coach. From the outset Bruce started to give me advice about specific training sessions. He also taught me the importance of thinking beyond the next race. Over the many years that followed we enjoyed discussing my training and racing programme as I built up towards key races.

In the summer of 1989 I decided – with Bruce's encouragement – to take up a part-time teaching job at Marlborough College, rather than pursue the career path towards which my university education had been leading. I had just won my

Bruce and Sue Tulloh, the two most important people in my running over the past 14 years

first international vest at the 1989 World Cross-Country Championships and was growing increasingly excited about my running. Due in no small part to Bruce's enthusiasm for my running, I was quickly able to make running more of a priority in my life.

Moving to Marlborough, where Bruce was also a schoolteacher, gave me the added advantage of being able to train under Bruce's close supervision. Some of my happiest memories go back to running over the Marlborough Downs in the early morning, after which I would end up at Bruce's house to do some stretching, before rushing back to my flat to shower in time for the start of morning lessons. In the afternoon I would join Bruce and Sue for a second workout either on the college fields or in the nearby woods. As we shared many hours of training together, they helped instil in me the confidence that I could compete at the highest level.

Training for the World Cup

After a short break following my first marathon in Hamburg (*see* pp. 20–23), I had just under five months to prepare for my next one – representing Britain at the World Cup Marathon in October 1993.* This was too long a time to concentrate on one race, so I decided to spend the first two months trying to improve my performances on the track. This would leave 11 weeks for me to prepare for the marathon.

Track racing in the summer

I had recovered well from the marathon in Hamburg, and two weeks after the race I resumed my normal routine of training. My two months of track competition that summer centred on two races. The first one, coming just seven weeks after my marathon in Hamburg, turned out to be a huge success. Taking advantage of the good base of endurance from all my marathon training and a few good track workouts after the Hamburg event, I ran a personal best time of 27:40 in the Bislett Games 10,000 m. For my second big race of the summer I decided to experiment with the idea of racing at sea-level on the same day as leaving altitude, in the hope of producing an equally good result in the Zurich 5000 m at the Weltklasse meeting in early August. But to no avail. After a good spell of preparation in a training camp in St Moritz, I ran a disappointing 13:37, finishing well down the field. After Zurich I finished off my short track season with a 3000 m race in the south of Germany, had a short holiday with friends on Lake Constance, and then returned home to start my build-up for the World Cup Marathon.

Altitude training

The timing of an athlete's descent from altitude can be crucial to success. Theories abound about the optimum time for competition at sea-level after completing a spell of training at altitude. For instance, many Kenyan runners who live at altitude prefer to race immediately after their descent – otherwise, as I once heard a Kenyan coach explaining, 'it's like gradually losing the fizz from an opened can of beer'. By contrast, the majority of European runners, myself included, have found that the best results come in the 10–20 day period after returning to sea-level.

*From 1985 to 1995, the IAAF World Cup Marathon took place every two years, as a separate event from the IAAF World Championships which encompassed the whole range of track and field disciplines. In addition to the individual race, the event involved a team competition; this was decided by the lowest aggregate finishing times of the first three runners from each country.

Getting focused

I now had 11 weeks to prepare for the race. It was time to get serious again about the marathon. Having spent much of the summer 'thinking track', the aim now was to 'think distance'. Since my first marathon had been run off an eight-week build-up (following a viral problem earlier in the year), for this marathon I felt I had time on my side so I deliberately held back in the intensity of my training for the first five weeks. There was no need to apply maximum effort from the start of the build-up; the really hard phase of the training would commence six weeks before the race.

With Bruce's help I planned two phases of hard training to prepare for the marathon. The first phase lasted five weeks and was done at sea-level. It was made up of consistently good weekly mileage for four weeks, followed by an easy week leading up to a half-marathon race. Then came the second and hardest phase of the training, where I spent three weeks at altitude. An easy week back home followed, leading up to a 10-mile race. By then the hard training was over and I was already starting to ease down for the marathon (*see* Table 2.4).

Table 2.4 Building up to the World Cup Marathon

Week	Relative intensity of training	Hard sessions	Total training volume
1	Moderate	Hill workout, 4 x 3 km road	184 km
2	Hard	38 km long run, 2 x (8 x 600 m) grass, fartlek	188 km
3	Hard	48 km long run, 15 km tempo run, hill workout	190 km
4	Moderate	4 x 4 km road, 6 x 1 km dirt road, 8 x 400 m track	172 km
5	Easy	39 km long run	104 km
6	Moderate	Half-marathon race, 40 km long run	194 km
7	Very hard	4 x 3 km grass, fartlek, 16 km tempo run	240 km
8	Very hard	10 x 1 km grass/track, 40 km long run	192 km
9	Easy	8 km tempo run, 16 x 200 m strides	160 km
Two weeks to go to marathon: 10-mile race followed by reduction in training			

Over the course of the build-up, I aimed first to increase the distance of the long run – for which pace was less important than duration. Then, having completed an 'over-distance' run of 30 miles, I switched my attention to improving the speed of these longer runs. By the end of the second phase of hard training I was running my long runs at close to race-pace effort. Table 2.5 illustrates how the speed, and therefore the toughness, of these runs increased as the race approached.

Table 2.5 Increasing the pace of the long run

Weeks before marathon	Length of run	Time (hours:min)	Pace (min/km)
11 weeks	30 km	2:00	4:00
10 weeks	38 km	2:32	4:00
8½ weeks	48 km	3:07	3:55
7 weeks	39 km	2:22	3:40
5 weeks	40 km	2:23	3.35
3 weeks	40 km	2:15	3:22

No holding back

My final phase of hard training started the day after the Great North Run on Tyneside, where I had finished third in a time of 1:01:53. I flew out to the Pyrenees for three weeks training at altitude, during which time I ran over 390 miles in 21 days. This represented an increase in volume of 10% on the training I had done in the first half of the build-up. (For a comparison of my weekly schedule in these two phases of the build-up, *see* Table 2.6.) Training at my hardest at this phase of the build-up, from six weeks to three weeks before the race, meant that my

Table 2.6 Comparison of weekly training cycles in the build-up

7-day training cycle – 1st half of build-up			7-day training cycle – 2nd half of build-up		
	Day	Session		Day	Session
1	a.m.	10 km steady	1	7.00 a.m.	7 km easy
	p.m.	4 x 3 km road, 3 min recovery		10.00 a.m.	16 km tempo run
				p.m.	8 km easy
2	a.m.	10 km easy	2	a.m.	18 km easy
	p.m.	6 km easy			
3	a.m.	38 km long run (2 hr 32 min)	3	7.00 a.m.	7 km easy
				10.00 a.m.	16 km steady + 6 x 200 m strides
				p.m.	8 km easy
4	a.m.	9 km easy	4	7.00 a.m.	7 km easy
	p.m.	13 km steady + 6 x 100 m strides		10.00 a.m.	10 x 1 km grass/track, 3 min recovery
				p.m.	10 km easy
5	a.m.	10 km steady	5	7.00 a.m.	8 km easy
	p.m.	18 km steady		10.00 a.m.	17 km steady + 8 x 100 m strides
6	a.m.	10 km steady	6	a.m.	16 km steady
	p.m.	2 x (8 x 600 m) grass, 1 min/5 min recovery		p.m.	8 km steady
7	a.m.	17 km easy	7	a.m.	40 km long run (2 hr 15 min)
	p.m.	11 km steady			
	Total	118 miles		Total	130 miles

confidence was high as I approached the final stages of my preparation. But it also meant that I had time to recover from these exertions, and be fully rested for when the race came.

Ready to race

'Do the Chinese really drink turtle blood or not?' This was the question on the lips of every athletics journalist as the teams arrived in San Sebastian on the eve of the race. Six weeks previously, at their National Championships in Beijing, Chinese female distance runners had rewritten the record books for the 1500 m, 3000 m and 10,000 m events. Now they had announced their intention of coming to race in the World Cup Marathon. Would another world-best be created at this distance?

To the dismay of attending journalists and television crews, the Chinese women helped themselves to a large plate of pasta – just like everyone else.

My race plan was to stay with the leaders until the closing stages, at which point I would make a decisive move. I would cover any attempts by my opponents to break clear in the first 20 miles of the race by increasing my pace, but without accelerating too fast. Unless the pace was very slow, the key to conserving energy for the race's final stages lay in even-paced running.

The race threw up little in the way of surprises. A leading pack of about 20 runners reached the halfway point in 1:04:52. Soon after passing halfway, the home favourite Diego Garcia increased the tempo in an attempt to break clear. But the chasing group covered his move, as they did a few kilometres later when the leading Kenyan in the race adopted a similar tactic.

Winning the World Cup Marathon race in San Sebastian in 1993 . . .

Dietary supplements

Dietary supplements are commonly used by elite athletes to enhance performance, as well as to diminish the risks associated with hard training and fatigue. Today, more than ever before, exceptional athletic performance is likely to arouse suspicions as to the legality of any such aids. (For example, in distance-running circles, there has been much speculation recently over the extent of use of the banned drug *erythropoietin* (EPO), which boosts the body's oxygen-carrying capacity.) On the eve of the the World Cup race in 1993 there was, not surprisingly, considerable interest in what the Chinese athletes may or may not have been using. For more information on ergogenic aids, *see* Chapter 4, p. 59.

From 30 km to 38 km I watched and waited. As we approached a slight uphill (leading into a tunnel under the hillside which brought us back into the town centre), I made a decisive move. Within the space of 500 m I had opened up a 10-second lead. From then on, it was a matter of hanging on until the finish – which I just managed to do, winning the race by a slender eight-second margin. I had made it hard for myself by injecting such a dramatic change of pace, but in the end it had paid off. My winning time was 2:10:03, though I felt I could have run faster still had the race been run differently. For now, victory and a championship title – Britain's first in the marathon for 19 years – was all that mattered.

. . . and later on the rostrum

3 Race-specific training
Building endurance and speed

The end product of any marathon-training plan should be good endurance. What is meant by the term 'endurance', and how do you go about acquiring it?

Building endurance

From the point of view of the marathon runner, you could think of endurance as the ability to cope with unreasonable levels of tiredness for an uncomfortably long period of time. In terms of the process of developing endurance, however, this need not be quite as painful as the description above implies. Time is on your side: remember the rule of building up gradually. Having a structure to your training is also important, since this will help you monitor your progress and grow in confidence as your fitness improves. Good training also involves striking the right balance between long, slow running and faster-paced efforts.

'You could think of endurance as the ability to cope with unreasonable levels of tiredness for an uncomfortably long period of time.'

Quality versus quantity

Many runners who decide to run a marathon are motivated by the thought of completing the course within a set time – for instance, improving on their previous best time or breaking the three-, four- or five-hour barrier for the distance. Setting yourself these kind of time goals means that you have to pay attention to the endurance aspect of your preparation – the ability simply to keep going – as well as to the speed at which you train.

The purpose of your weekly long run, together with maintaining a good overall volume of miles run each week, is to develop endurance. Beyond a certain amount of long, slow running, however, your fitness will further improve only if you introduce some faster-paced running into your training programme. In the context of training for a marathon, these 'speed' sessions have little to do with flat-out sprinting. Some are designed to improve your 10 km running speed, while others are intended to improve your efficiency at running at your marathon pace. In other words, they are tailored towards preparing you specifically for certain races. As a mid-term goal for the first half of your marathon build-up, you should be aiming to run a half-marathon. To this end, the best training pace for your sessions of faster running is your 10 km race-pace. In the second half of your

The Yellow Pages Reading Half-Marathon is a good build-up race for a spring marathon

build-up, however, the emphasis should switch towards running closer to your marathon race-pace. (This is discussed in more detail on p. 42.)

There will always be a trade-off between quality and quantity. A higher overall weekly mileage, or a longer endurance run, will leave you with less energy to run well in your faster-paced workouts. This chapter should help you understand how best to achieve this balance between fast and slow running.

Establishing a weekly training routine

Developing fitness involves a continual cycle of stress and recovery. First you subject yourself to a certain level of stress, and then you allow yourself time to recover before progressing to a greater level of stress – all within the limits of your individual capability. You can think of this process as occurring both on a day-to-day basis and over a longer period – hence the importance of phases of hard *and* easy training described on p. 27. In terms of structuring a weekly training routine, you should intersperse days of moderate or hard effort with days of either light training or rest.

Starting with your weekly long run (which for most people takes place at the weekend), you should aim to do two more hard sessions in the course of a week's training. Whereas the effort involved in the long run comes from its duration, in the other two hard efforts it comes from faster-paced running.

Depending on your level of fitness, the rhythm of your training week might look something like this:

Table 3.1 Typical rhythm of a training week

Sunday	Monday	Tuesday	Wednesday	Thursday	Friday	Saturday
Long run	Easy or rest	Hard effort	Easy	Hard effort	Easy or rest	Steady

Your Thursday and Saturday sessions can be interchangeable – people in work might find that they have more time and energy for a harder session on Saturday. On the other hand, to ensure that you are fresh and well-rested for a big effort in your long run on Sunday, you might prefer to do your second hard session earlier in the week. Use a programme that fits in best around your lifestyle, enabling you to perform well in your hard efforts as well as to recover well afterwards.

Let's now look in more detail at the nature of your harder sessions.

The long run: 'time on your feet'

The single most important component of your training programme is the weekly long run. Over the course of a marathon build-up, you should aim to increase the duration of this run so that towards the end of your build-up you are running for a good proportion of the time it will take you to complete the marathon itself. I say 'duration' rather than 'distance', because the speed of these runs is less important than how long they last. So, at least in the early stages of the build-up, you might prefer to quantify these long runs in terms of 'time on your feet' rather than as a certain distance.

In the early stages of the build-up to my first marathon, I was struggling to carry out my normal load of training without becoming excessively tired. In place of my usual long run of 18–20 miles (which I would normally run in under two hours), my coach therefore suggested that I went out for some 'long jogs' (walking interspersed with light running) of up to three hours' duration. In these training efforts I would cover around 25 miles – admittedly, at a lower level of effort than for my usual long run. Still, these long slow runs gave me a training benefit. They also helped me get used to the thought of just how far 26 miles actually was, coming from a racing background where six miles was considered to be part of 'long-distance running'.

How long and how far?

The length or duration of your long run will depend on:

- your current level of fitness – beginners, for example, who have followed the training outlined in Chapter 1, should aim to walk/run for at least an hour at the start of their build-up, and increase this to three hours as they approach the race;
- the time and energy available to you;
- the stage you are at in your build-up;
- your expected finishing time in the marathon.

Obviously, the fitter you are, the further you should be able to run. On the other hand, if you expect to take five hours to complete your marathon, it makes sense to do at least one long effort during the course of your build-up of three hours minimum.

Broadly speaking, your long weekly effort should last between two and three hours. If you try to run for longer than three hours on a regular basis, you run the risk of over-exhaustion. (More advanced runners may decide to do one of their long training runs over a course of more than 26 miles. But I recommend this only for those who can cover this distance in training in not much more than three hours. The benefit of this kind of run is as much psychological as physical.)

Once you have reached the point where you are confident of keeping going for two hours or more, you might then want to think about how *far* you are running. Beginners should attempt at least one run of 18–20 miles before the marathon; more advanced runners should aim to do four or five runs of 20 miles or more. (My coach has devised the following rule-of-thumb: if the total distance of your five longest runs over the course of your build-up to a marathon amounts to 100 miles or more, you should feel well prepared for the event.) How this distance is gradually increased over the course of a build-up is illustrated in Table 2.3 on p. 26.

Your longest runs, just like your heaviest weeks of training, should come in the third quarter of your build-up – between six and three weeks before your marathon. To reduce the risk of injury, resist the temptation of attempting very long runs too early in the build-up, unless they are in the form of long 'hikes'. You should also leave sufficient time between your last long training run and the marathon itself, to ensure that you have fully recovered from the exertions of training. This means that your last really long run (18 miles or more) should be done three weeks before your marathon. (If you have missed a considerable amount of training earlier in the build-up, you might resort to doing this run at the latest two weeks before the marathon.)

Introducing some faster-paced running

In the early stages of your build-up, the focus of these sessions should be simply to run at a faster tempo than your normal 'steady' running pace, over relatively short distances. (For a definition of 'steady' running, *see* Chapter 1, p. 11.) Sessions of short, faster running will add variety to your weekly routine of training. Instead of lapsing into a plod every time you go out to train, you will be able to focus on making sustained efforts during the course of a given workout, punctuated with short periods of recovery. These sessions play as important a role in raising your level of fitness as will an increase in your overall volume of training.

Most runners tend to get more out of a varied training programme – where the variety comes from doing your training runs at different speeds and with different degrees of effort. Your marathon training will therefore include the following sessions of faster-paced running.

- A 'repetition' session (e.g. 4 x 5 min with 3 min recovery) – this involves making a hard effort for five minutes of fast running, followed by a recovery of three minutes of slow jogging (or walking). This cycle is repeated three more times. How fast you run in each individual section (or 'interval') of the workout depends on the overall length of the session. Since you should aim to run each repetition at roughly the same speed, it is important that you spread your effort over the entire workout. As you get tired towards the end of the session you might have to make more of an effort to maintain the same running pace as at the start.

- A simpler variation of combined fast and slow running is a 'fartlek' (literally meaning 'speed-play') session. Here, you alternate fast and slow running – either according to feeling (a *spontaneous fartlek*) or, as many runners prefer, with reference to time or distance (a *structured fartlek,* e.g. 1 min fast/1 min easy, or 6 lampposts fast/4 easy).
- A 'pace run' or 'tempo run', which involves a longer, sustained effort of brisk running without reaching maximum speed. Ideally, this should be run over a set distance – perhaps on a quiet stretch of road that you have measured beforehand by car or bike. In these sessions you will practise the art of maintaining a strong running pace over a longer period. From them you should also develop a sense of pace judgement which will prove useful when it comes to running your marathon.
- A session of fast strides (e.g. 6–8 x 150 m), at the end of a steady run. Here you are running close to your maximum speed without actually sprinting.

More information on building speed into your training is given on p. 42 of this chapter – *Race pace.*

Monitor and modify

As your training progresses, increased fitness levels might leave you feeling that you need less recovery time between each hard session. Remember, however, that your hard workouts will actually become more demanding as you get closer to your marathon. You will also be running more miles each week and covering more miles on your weekly long run. So resist the urge to do much more than your programme for the week allows.

On the other hand, you may find that you are struggling to cope with the overall intensity of your training. If this is the case, it is probably better to reduce the number of hard efforts each week rather than run them at a lower level of effort. You can modify your training programme in the following ways:

- in place of a hard session, run a 'half-session' of a steady run plus strides;
- if you're not yet recovered in time for your next hard session, give yourself another day;
- remember that sometimes you may derive more benefit from having a complete day off running than from going out for a slow plod.

Your performance in the marathon is the product of weeks of good training, so one fewer hard session will hardly make a difference. It is better to be consistent with your training and feel good about it, than let it get the better of you. So learn to be flexible with your training programme and adapt it to suit your individual requirements.

Race pace – building speed

As you get nearer to your marathon, you should have a growing sense that your reserves of endurance are being brought to their peak. You should derive confidence from knowing that you are able to handle greater volumes of training than at the start of your build-up, and that you have gradually increased the length of your weekly long run.

What about the progression of your sessions of faster running? In your sessions of repetition and tempo running you should be thinking about running further rather than faster: you should aim to develop your ability to maintain a good running pace over increasingly longer distances.

Remember that training should be specific to the event. As you begin to concentrate your thoughts on running your marathon, during the second half of your build-up, you will benefit by doing some of your training runs at a pace that more closely approximates your intended running speed in the marathon itself.

The sessions described below – in the form of 'repetitions' run over shorter intervals, and 'tempo runs' over slightly longer distances – show the kind of progression that your training should follow over the course of a build-up.

Repetitions and tempo runs

Repetitions

- *First-time marathoners:* three months before your marathon you might be able to run 4 x 1 km (or 4 x 5 minutes), with three minutes recovery, at your 10 km pace. Six weeks later you should be fit enough to attempt 3 x 8–10 minutes, with three minutes recovery, at around half-marathon pace.
- *Advanced runners:* progressing from 3 x 3 km, with three minutes recovery, at your 10-mile race pace to 2 x 5–6 km, with four minutes recovery, at your marathon pace.

In other words, as your training progresses, the emphasis shifts towards running fast over longer intervals. Short recovery periods more closely approximate the feeling of the sustained effort required in running a marathon, so it is better to reduce the recovery time rather than increase the running speed of the faster sections.

Tempo runs (or pace runs)

- *First-time marathoners:* three months before your marathon you might attempt a tempo run of three miles at slightly slower than 10 km race pace. Six weeks later you might be ready to do a tempo run of between five and six miles at just below half-marathon pace.
- *Advanced runners:* three months before, a tempo run of 4–5 miles; six weeks later a tempo run of 8–10 miles.

The pace of your tempo runs should be 'brisk, yet controlled'. Remind yourself of the purpose of the workout: to rehearse your race effort. With the exception of the elite, there is no need to attempt very long tempo runs.

Stay within your limits

Once you have done a few sessions of repetition and tempo running, you should start to get an idea of how fast you are running even without having to look at your watch. You should aim to run as relaxed and efficiently as possible, with a view to maintaining an even pace over an extended distance. The toughness of the session comes also from having to concentrate on making a more sustained effort.

Running economy

Take a look at the world's best marathon runners, and you will notice certain general features of their style of running. Their neck and shoulders remain relaxed even as their body grows tired. Their arms are held loosely near to their waist and use up minimal energy. Since they use a short, quick stride pattern, they have a relatively low knee lift. These features broadly constitute what is known as 'running economy' – a style of running that allows you to conserve energy over a long period. The more you are able to run with such efficiency, the greater will be your chances of success at the marathon. (Note too that physical efficiency is complimented by exercising mental restraint in running your marathon – *see Useful tips* on planning a race strategy, pp. 73–74.)

Running efficiently up and down hills: when running downhill, try to lean slightly forwards and carry your arms low at your side, only using them if necessary to keep your balance. When running uphill, move more on to your toes, shorten your stride and use your arms in a brisk forward-and-back motion to sustain your speed.

Variations on a theme

The one drawback of the tempo run in training is that it is often difficult to maintain effort and concentration for an extended period – especially if you're running alone. If this is the case, you can achieve a similar training effect by breaking the distance into shorter segments run with only short (1–2 min) recoveries. For example:

- *First-time marathoners:* a four-mile continuous run (around 35 min) can be replaced with a session of 2 x 2 miles (around 16–18 min) with a 2-minute recovery after the first effort.
- *Advanced runners:* an eight-mile tempo run can be replaced with 3M-2M-3M with a 1–2 minute recovery.

As with the repetition sessions above, the short recoveries ensure that the whole workout feels like one continuous effort – although you have the benefit of being able to concentrate on one section at a time. For the elite runner, you can replace

Josiah Thugwane (17) and Stefano Baldini (23) display an efficient running action in the latter stages of the 1997 London Marathon

a short jog recovery with a segment of reduced-intensity running. Thus a 15 km tempo run might be done as a continuous cycle of five efforts, each comprising 2 km at marathon pace followed by 1 km at 30 seconds slower than marathon pace.

The structure of your marathon training should enable you to improve your ability to run further at a given speed (rather than to run faster at a set distance – though as you get fitter, you will quite likely achieve both these goals). Feeling strong rather than speedy is the best way to develop a sense of readiness for competition.

Remember too, as your training progresses, to 'hasten slowly'. Try to stay on top of your training, and pace yourself through the various stages of your build-up. A sense of *timing* – in terms of bringing yourself to a peak of physical and mental readiness – is crucial for good performance.

Pay attention both to the speed of your runs and to the distance covered.
Intersperse harder sessions of training with days of rest or easy running.
Measure your long run by time, not by distance.
Extend your range of distance over the course of the build-up.
Practise running for a sustained effort at close to your marathon race-pace.
Reduce the recovery intervals within sessions as you get closer to the race.
Try to bring yourself to a peak of fitness at the right time.

Useful tips

Race-specific training – devising training routes

Some of your main training efforts during your marathon build-up – for instance, running at a constant pace over an extended distance, or practising taking drinks during a long run – can be made easier if you give some thought to *where* you run these sessions. Here are a few useful considerations, followed by some information on how I have devised routes for key sessions performed during the build-up to some of my marathons.

- What is the nature of the terrain?
- Will you be affected by traffic?
- How can you measure the route?
- Is there any protection from the wind?
- How can I arrange to take drinks during my run?

- *Practising a constant pace over an extended period* (e.g. 3 x 10 min). It might help to seek out stretches of preferably flat and relatively traffic-free running. I have used a range of venues for this, including riverside towpaths, disused airfields and dirt roads through forests. On quiet but wide country roads I have also run sessions accompanied (at a distance of 10–20 m behind) by someone on a bike or in a car, to alert other vehicles to my presence.
- *Repetitions over kilometres/miles.* Measure out your course beforehand by bike (if running on a traffic-free dirt road) or by car. Where possible choose a relatively sheltered area, which might allow you to run the course in both directions while keeping your times/effort constant.
- *Practising the art of holding yourself back.* Use a lap course (e.g. three laps of a 10 km route for a long 30 km run), and try to increase your speed over each consecutive lap – saving your biggest effort for the end of the session.
- *Taking drinks on the run* (remember that you want to drink once every half-hour during a 2½ hr run). Here, you might have to rely on a coach or friend to accompany you on a bike or in a car. Alternatively, use a 'loop' course which allows you to take a drink (set up beforehand) at the same point on each loop. Ideally, you might benefit from both options.

Using races to monitor your progress

By the time you start your marathon build-up, you should have some experience of what it's like to take part in a race – perhaps you've just completed a local fun run, or maybe you've even got your first half-marathon behind you.

Taking part in a race gives you a different kind of experience from simply going out for a training run. You learn to cope with pre-race nerves as you line up at the start with crowds of other runners. In the race itself it is important that you exercise good pace judgement, resisting for instance the temptation to start too quickly. Similarly, nothing in training can quite compare with that post-race feeling of satisfaction and relief from having completed the course.

As well as becoming more familiar with the race-specific experience, doing some races in the course of your build-up can further your preparation for the marathon in a number of ways.

- *Races represent useful short-term goals and serve to break up the slog of training.* For instance, you might aim to run a 10-mile race after one month of your build-up, and a half-marathon at the end of the second month.
- *A good race performance can give a boost to your training.* You start to see the fruits of your training, and once you have recovered from your race you can resume your normal training with renewed vigour.
- *Races further develop your fitness.* Harder than any exertion you may make in training, racing places greater stress on your system, so you may need longer to recover than after a hard training session. You should not plan to race more than twice a month during your build-up, otherwise you will have too many interruptions to your normal training routine.
- *Races help you to 'rest'.* Being obsessive creatures, many runners are notoriously bad at allowing themselves an easy week of training. Races are one way of ensuring that you plan one or two periods of lighter training into your build-up. Remember that you are more likely to perform well in a race if you have rested well in the few days beforehand – a pattern you should follow even if you are treating the race as part of training towards a longer-term goal.
- *Races will help you determine a realistic target for your marathon race-pace.* For instance, if you can run 10 miles in under 69 minutes, or a half-marathon in around 92 minutes (7:00 min/mile), then your target race pace for the marathon would be around 7:30-7:40 min/mile. My coach has a method for predicting the finishing time in the marathon, based on performances at the half-marathon. This involves doubling the half-marathon time and then adding 7.5%. As an example, if your half-marathon time is 1:31:30, your goal for the marathon might be (91.5 x 2) + 7.5% = 3:16.

Below is an example of how I used a 10-mile race to monitor my progress as I built up towards the 1997 London Marathon.

Before starting my build-up to the 1997 London Marathon, I had done a couple of tough cross-country races on the continent. Thereafter I did only one more race, halfway through the really hard period of training and six weeks before the marathon itself. The event I chose was the Woking 10-Mile race, a popular event for runners preparing for the London Marathon. Woking is conveniently situated only about a half-hour's drive from our home. The proximity of the race venue meant that I minimised the stress of travelling to and from the competition.

The race was usually won in a time of around 50 minutes. My training up to this point in my build-up indicated that I was capable of running between 46:30 and 47:00 minutes, so I was not expecting to meet much serious opposition. Nevertheless, I wanted to run hard, feel confident about the progress of my training, and ensure a good last race before the marathon. I therefore planned an easier week of training leading up to the event, reducing the volume of my training in race-week by about a third and holding off from doing any really hard workouts.

Soon after arriving in Woking on the morning of the race, I discovered that four top Kenyan athletes were running. Apparently, they were due to compete in the Los Angeles Marathon that weekend but had been unable to get visas to travel from London to the States, so were stuck in Britain and looking for competition. I was glad that I had eased down to be sufficiently fresh to take them on! With the added incentive of chasing my own course record from two years previously, I ran away to victory in a time of 46:29, beating the old record by just six seconds. It was a nice tonic to my build-up, with an even harder three-week cycle of training ahead of me.

Training for the Olympic Marathon

Six months before the 1996 Olympic Marathon I arrived in Boulder, Colorado, to start my preparation for the race. I moved into an apartment with two other running friends, Jon Brown and Tommy Ratcliffe.

Keeping good company

Over the next seven weeks the three of us enjoyed each other's company and had a good spell of training together. We often ran with a group of Kenyans who were living in the same block of apartments. We had a physiotherapist on-hand to give us regular treatment. While there, we came into contact with the German coach Dieter Hogan, who passed on to us his ideas on marathon training. Dieter was coach and partner to Uta Pippig, who at the time was ranked no. 1 in the world at the marathon. His coaching expertise had developed from working alongside the coach to Waldemar Cierpinski, who had won the Olympic marathon in 1976 and 1980. More recently, his coaching skills had helped Uta achieve a string of marathon victories, including wins in Berlin and Boston and a 2:21:45 clocking.

As my marathon career had progressed, I felt increasingly able to handle greater volumes of training. Between 1989 and 1992 my weekly mileage as an international 10,000 m runner had been around 110–120 miles. From 1993 onwards I had started to reach higher weekly volumes, regularly exceeding 130 miles of running per week and occasionally covering as much as 150 miles per week. Clearly, there had had to be some trade-off between quality and quantity: though my endurance had developed, I had found it increasingly difficult to retain my speed over shorter distances. All my best times for distances between 3 km and 10 km had been set in 1993 or earlier.

Finding the right balance

Dieter's training regime included conventional components of marathon training, such as sessions at 10 km pace (e.g. 7 x 1 mile or 10 x 1 km), fartlek and strides over 100–400 m, and long runs over 20–25 miles. The emphasis of Dieter's training approach, however, lay with the continuous tempo runs of 15 km and 25 km. Dieter reasoned that these sustained efforts, more than any other form of training, came closest to simulating the demands of the marathon. The aim of these workouts was to increase the pace gradually over the course of the run, so that towards the end of the session we were running at – or faster than – marathon-race speed. (This same principle was also applied to some of the longer 25-mile runs, especially in the latter stage of a marathon build-up.) Taken together with the 10 km training sessions, Dieter's programme ensured that neither speed nor endurance was neglected. The only question was whether we would be able to cope with the overall intensity of the training load.

Knowing how tough his own methods were, Dieter regularly gave out instructions on how we should eat, drink, and rest to enable us to cope with the training. Coming from a tradition where the path to high achievement had been narrowed down to a precise science, much attention was paid to detail. Admittedly, there were occasions when Dieter failed to appreciate important cultural differences – such as when he tried to persuade the Kenyan runners to use wholemeal flour (not widely available in Kenya) to make their *ugali*! But on the whole, much of what Dieter preached seemed to make sense. More importantly, his results demonstrated that his methods worked.

By the end of my first seven weeks, I was beginning to feel a different athlete to the one who had been seen trailing miserably behind Jon, my training partner, in a session during the early weeks of our stay. My confidence had been restored, and after an eight-month break from competition I got ready to run my first race since having surgery the previous autumn. (The background to this injury is given in Chapter 7, p. 100.) On my return to Britain, I ran a series of road races to test my fitness. I quickly discovered how well things were going when in a half-marathon in Paris in mid-April, I recorded a personal best time of 1:01:06.

Sensing how well my training had gone during my seven weeks in Boulder, I planned a second stint of training there for the main part of my final three-month build-up to the Olympic Marathon later that summer.

Countdown to Atlanta

I started my build-up in earnest 12 weeks before the marathon. I spent the first two weeks training in Marlborough, where Bruce and Sue's assistance enabled me to recreate some of the benefits – in the form of coaching support and massage – of the training-camp environment. I then flew back out to Boulder for a block of eight weeks' training at altitude. *En route* I had an overnight stop in Atlanta, which gave me the chance to have another run over the marathon course.

The summer in Colorado was a far cry from the snow and icy cold we had experienced earlier in the year. Now, temperatures would rise regularly into the mid-thirties, which helped me develop the habit of replacing lost fluids during and after training.

During the next two months my training progressed better than I could have hoped. Six weeks prior to the marathon I ran a half-marathon in similar conditions to those expected in Atlanta. In a close sprint-finish I just failed to win the race, but in view of the hilly nature of the course still felt pleased with my finishing time of 1:03:01. I returned to Boulder for the final phase of hard training. The schedule for those final three weeks at altitude was tougher than any I had previously experienced. I knew I was taking risks in exploring new limits to my training capacity. For instance, over one four-day period I did two 22-mile long runs and a 10 km speed workout of 7 x 1 mile. (*See* Table 3.2.)

Table 3.2 Comparison of weekly training cycles – build-up to half-marathon (April) and marathon (August)

	7-day training cycle – build-up to half-marathon (April 1996)			7-day training cycle – build-up to marathon (August 1996)	
	Day	Session		Day	Session
1	a.m.	35 km long run	1	a.m.	35 km long run
2	a.m.	15 km easy	2	a.m.	18 km easy
	p.m.	15 km steady		p.m.	8 km steady + strides
3	a.m.	16 km steady	3	early a.m.	8 km easy
	p.m.	11 km easy + strides		a.m.	7 x 1 mile, 3 min recovery
				p.m.	10 km easy
4	a.m.	15 km tempo run	4	a.m.	35 km long run
	p.m.	8 km easy			
5	a.m.	25 km steady	5	a.m.	14 km easy
	p.m.	12 km steady		p.m.	10 km easy
6	a.m.	17 km steady	6	a.m.	16 km steady
	p.m.	8 km easy		p.m.	9 km easy + strides
7	a.m.	5 x 1 mile, 2 min recovery	7	early a.m.	8 km easy
	p.m.	10 km easy		a.m.	25 km tempo run
	Total	130 miles		**Total**	138 miles

Using the time between the hard sessions to rest and recover as best I could, I somehow managed to get through the training without breaking down. At the start of my taper, 2½ weeks prior to the race, I began to feel stronger and more determined than ever before.

The final part of my preparation and an account of the race in Atlanta are described in Chapter 5, pp. 77–80.

Peaking for the London Marathon

By the end of 1996 I had run six marathons, four of which were championship races. My record included a win in the 1993 World Cup Marathon, fifth place in the 1996 Olympic Marathon in Atlanta, and a personal best time of 2:10:03. Top of my list of priorities for post-Olympic year was to improve my best time for the distance. Having never yet run in Britain's premier road race, there was no better occasion on which to attempt this than the 1997 London Marathon.

I had been over the London Marathon course many times previously – twice on the back of a motorbike when I had worked for the BBC commentary team, and on other occasions when I had trained on stretches of the course. Once, at 5.00 a.m. on a rainy, wind-swept Sunday in late October, I had run the first 21 miles of the marathon route with my wife Gail following behind in the car. Now, for the first time, I would be racing over the complete course – every mile of which, unlike any other marathon I had run, would be very familiar to me.

Preparation

In my preparation for the Olympic Marathon during the summer of 1996, I had discovered new limits to my training (see pp. 49–50). The challenge now was to reproduce that form for my debut in London. After getting married and moving house to Teddington in September 1996, I returned to training at the start of October. As the winter approached I made my customary trip to Kenya for a spell of altitude training, and on my return home in mid-January I ran a couple of cross-country races to see how my fitness was progressing. Then, with 10 weeks remaining to the marathon, I started to focus my energies on preparing for the race in London.

Aware of the demands of heavy marathon training, I planned to do the bulk of my hard training in a training camp, away from the distractions of home. In the second week of February I headed out to the Italian Olympic Training Centre at Tirrenia on the Mediterranean.

During the months of December and January my training had been geared towards cross-country races over 10 km. Out in Italy I started to shift the emphasis towards greater volumes of training, and sessions of tempo running that would get me used to the sustained effort required in running a marathon. The following seven weeks were divided into two blocks of training, each comprising a phase of hard training followed by one recovery week. The first phase of hard training lasted three weeks. Each week included a long run of between 2¼ and 2¾ hours; a session designed to improve my speed over 10 km; and a tempo run over an extended distance (see Table 3.3).

Table 3.3 The first phase of marathon-specific training

Week	Hard sessions	Weekly mileage
1	10 km cross-country race, 22 M long run, 25 km tempo run	104
2	29 M long run, 20 km tempo run, 15 km fartlek	150
3	24 M long run, 3 x 6 km road, 8 x 1 km grass/track	132

At the end of this block of training I returned home for a week of easy training followed by a 10-mile road race in Woking (*see* also p. 47). Two days after the race I was back in Tirrenia for the second phase of hard training.

Race simulation

The key sessions over the following three weeks involved doing a lot of running at marathon race-speed (*see* Table 3.4). To ensure that I did not overdo the training at this stage, there still had to be a variety of paces at which I trained. But the nearer I got to the race, the more I wanted to rehearse the kind of effort and imagine the kind of tiredness that I would need to endure in the marathon itself.

In the week after my race in Woking, I did a sustained hard effort over 20 km where the tempo alternated between a 'fast' (3:00 min/km) pace and a 'cruise' (3:12 min/km) pace – since my target race-pace for the marathon was 3:02 min/km. The following week I ran the last 10 km of the 40 km long run in 32:20 (3:14 min/km), which, in the context of a heavy period of training, simulated race-pace effort. My last hard session in Tirrenia was a 25 km tempo run at progressively faster speeds, starting at 3:14 min/km (16:10 for the first 5 km) and finishing at 3:01 min/km (15:05 for the last 5 km).

When this second phase of hard training was over (at the start of Week 7), there were just under four weeks to go to the race. I returned home and had a few days of easy running before attempting two more tough sessions. Three weeks before the marathon I ran a 30 km time-trial in 1:32:18 (under 2:10:00 marathon pace). Four days later I ran a 15 km tempo run on dirt and road, including five 2 km to 1 km pace changes, in 44:46.

Table 3.4 The second phase – training at marathon race-pace

Week	Hard sessions	Weekly mileage
4	35 km long run, then 6 easy days before race	95
5	10 mile race, 39 km long run, 20 km tempo run	140
6	40 km long run, 10 x 1 km track, 25 km tempo run	152
7	41 km long run, five easy days, 30 km tempo run	106
8	15 km tempo run, 20 x 400 m track	108

I now knew I was in great shape. Assuming my final two weeks of preparation went well, I would be ready to perform at my best in London.

The final stage of preparation for competition is the topic of Chapter 5 (pp. 68–80); the outcome of my race in London is described in Chapter 6 (pp. 89–92).

4 Lifestyle matters

Diet, rest and recovery

'Training,' one American coach once told me, 'is a 24-hour proposition.' Even if you struggle to live up to this standard, you can still heed the idea behind the words: if you want to get the most out of your running, you need to think about how your style of living fits around your running.

Very few of you will become full-time professional athletes for whom running *is* your life. On the other hand, if you're serious about your quest for fitness, then your whole approach to training has to become more than just an occasional hobby – and certainly so in the build-up to a marathon. It has to become part of your everyday routine, even if this pattern of living lasts only for a short while. This chapter looks at two important aspects of life outside training – diet and rest – that can contribute significantly to successful athletic performance. It is outside the scope of this book to give comprehensive information on sports nutrition – only the basic principles are addressed here. For more detailed advice, refer to a good sports nutrition guide, such as *The Complete Guide to Sports Nutrition* by Anita Bean (A & C Black).

Eat well, train well

You require energy to live, and you need even more of it when you start to train hard. At its most basic level, this explains why you need to pay attention to your diet as a marathon runner. The more you train, the more food you need to eat. Remember the African saying: 'an empty sack won't stand up'.

However, a good diet is not just about eating the right quantity of food. You should also be eating a wide range of the right kind of foods. In this regard also, the African runner sets us a good example by following a diet that is high in carbohydrate, low in fat, and includes moderate amounts of protein. The pattern of their diet is ideal for providing the energy needs necessary for world-class performance.

'Remember the African saying: "an empty sack won't stand up".'

A healthy diet has much in common with a good training regime, in the following ways.

- First, eating well should become part of your routine. Adopting a good diet – eating a piece of fruit at every meal, for example, or using semi-skimmed milk in place of whole milk – should be as commonplace as showering and stretching after your morning run.

- Second, vary your diet. Just as you need to do a variety of sessions in training to prepare for a marathon, so when it comes to diet you need to eat a wide range of good foods. There's no such thing as the one best meal for runners. It's more a matter of getting the right balance in the overall pattern of your eating.
- Third, be sensible about what you can and can't eat. Apply the same commonsense approach to your diet as you do to your training. It's not good to exist solely on chocolate or ice cream, but there's no harm in eating them in moderation. It's more important to eat enough of the right kind of foods than deny yourself those small sweet things that – taken in moderation – will not adversely effect your performance.

What is the runner's diet?

To answer this question, it's first important to have some basic understanding of how the body's fuel system works. Your body's energy requirements are met by two main sources: fat and carbohydrate. In the chemical reactions that take place within your body to produce energy (known as the ATP metabolic pathway), carbohydrate – or glycogen, the form in which it is stored in your body – is more immediately available than fat to meet your energy needs. This puts a premium on replenishing your glycogen stores both during and after bouts of hard training.

To do this you need first to ensure that your diet contains a good supply of carbohydrates – around 60–70% of your energy intake. When I am in hard training, or during the so-called 'carbo-loading' phase of a marathon build-up (*see* p. 56), I aim to eat about 600 g of carbohydrate per day – or roughly 10 g per day for every kg of body weight. In normal training, the amount may be around 400–500 g, which is still considerably above that found in the average western diet (200–300 g). Popular sources of carbohydrate-rich foods are bread, pasta, potatoes, rice and breakfast cereal.

Second, you should consider taking glucose-rich drinks during your long runs in training and in the marathon itself to conserve your stores of glycogen. Remember that low levels of glycogen will require your body to utilise fat as fuel; and because of the relatively low rate at which fat can be used by the working muscles, this will cause you to slow down.

Beware, however, of adopting too extreme a solution. You may shed a few more pounds in weight by reducing the amount of fat in your diet, but some fat is needed by your body for the process of muscle repair. So a small amount of fat – between 10–20% of your energy intake for the serious athlete – is both inevitable and essential in a healthy diet.

Certain fats are better for you than others. Cut down on foods that are high in saturated fats – such as crisps, biscuits, fried food, full-fat dairy produce, butter and sauces such as mayonnaise – but be more relaxed about consuming the kind of unsaturated fats found in fish and plants (e.g. olive oil, sunflower seed oil).

The remaining 15–20% of your diet should be made up of protein. Proteins play an important part in your body's process of recovery after intense training. Again, it comes down to a question of variety and balance in your diet. You may be able to get your daily protein requirements from eating a large steak every day, but this might also result in you comsuming too much fat and not enough carbohydrate. In addition to meat and poultry, good supplies of protein are found in fish, milk and cheese, eggs and pulses (e.g. tofu and soya beans).

Unlike race-horse jockeys before a race, or boxers before their next bout, runners in training don't need to watch their weight too carefully. If you are overweight at the start of your training programme, you will soon begin to shed pounds as you take more exercise. Once you have discovered an optimum training weight, it may then be helpful to check your weight on a weekly basis to ensure that you are neither eating too much nor too little (*see* above).

Remember also the importance of drinking after exercise. Dehydration can occur from having drunk too little either before or during the course of training. For every hour of exercise you should aim to drink 1–1½ litres over and above your normal amount. (This amount should increase if you are training in unusually warm weather.) A dark yellow colour in your urine, coupled often with a significant loss of weight, is a sign that you aren't drinking enough.

The great thing about being a runner is that you burn off lots of calories when you exercise. This means that you should be eating more than the average sedentary person and that you need not become obsessed with the exact quantities of different types of food that you are eating. The key thing is to develop healthy habits in your overall pattern of shopping, cooking and eating. Eating well will make you feel good and at the same time benefit your training.

Fitting meals around exercise

Just as you need to plan when you are going to train, so too you need to think about when you are going to eat – both before and after exercise. The rule of thumb is not to eat anything in the two-hour period before going out for a run, and if this is a larger meal it's better to leave a gap of three to four hours. Many runners find that an early morning run before breakfast is a good time to train, or in the early evening before dinner. Conversely, don't deprive yourself of food for the whole day and then expect to feel good on your evening run. If you do prefer to train in the second half of the day, make sure you have a good breakfast and if necessary an easily digestible snack later on so as to maintain your energy levels throughout the day.

Sample meal plan, 1 day of marathon training

Breakfast: glass of orange juice, cereal + banana + semi-skimmed milk, toast + margarine (or other low-fat spread) + honey/marmalade, tea/coffee
Morning snack*: apple, fruit tea
Lunch: sandwich of ham/cheese + tomato, low-fat yoghurt, kiwi fruit, glass of water
Afternoon snack*: English muffin + jam, cup of tea
Dinner: Spinach leaf salad, grilled fish + rice + broccoli, slice of carrot cake and camomile tea

*Snacks optional depending on time of workout and phase of training

Post-exercise nutrition

Having accepted that there's no magic food that will make you run faster, it's still worth considering how your diet can contribute to your performance. For instance, the best way to speed recovery after a hard bout of training is to start the refuelling process within the first two hours (and preferably within the first hour) of finishing exercise. Try to develop the habit of following your run with at least a small snack (e.g. some toast, or a piece of cake or muffin) and a large glass of water or juice. Bananas are also popular among runners wanting to replenish their energy stores quickly and efficiently. If you're training away from home, it may be useful to take with you a small post-run snack (e.g. some fruit or an energy bar and a drink) which will help revive you after exercise and keep you going until your next proper meal.

Pre-race carbo-loading

'Carbo-loading' before a marathon*

It is crucial that you start your marathon with maximal reserves of glycogen. This is because the amount of glycogen that your body can access from its reserves in the course of a marathon may actually be less than you need to complete a marathon. Your body accounts for the shortfall partly by drawing on fat as a source of fuel – providing about 10% of the energy requirement for elite athletes, and rising to nearer 50% among slower runners – and partly by using supplementary amounts of carbohydrate that you consume while running your marathon (*see* below).

Building up your carbohydrate reserves before a race is known as 'carbo-loading'. Although the term is commonly associated with pasta parties on the evening before a marathon, the process should start about three days before your race. If your marathon is on a Sunday, lunch and dinner on both the Friday and Saturday should be carbohydrate-rich meals. The emphasis should be on eating a good helping of carbohydrate, but not stuffing yourself or overeating to the extent that you are left with a bloated feeling when you go to the start. When carbo-loading, you should also take on board plenty of fluid – without this, your body is unable to fill your glycogen stores.

Pre-race eating

It's important to be careful about your diet before racing – or indeed, before a particularly hard workout. The intensity of effort involved in racing, coupled with the nervous tension that accompanies any competitive situation, can unsettle

---

*A small minority of elite marathon runners no longer use the method of carbo-loading before a marathon. Either they have reservations about eating too much in the period leading up to the event, or they feel confident that in the course of regular hard training they have learned how to refuel adequately after exhausting their glycogen stores. However, the practice of carbo-loading – as I advocate here – is still common among first-time marathon runners and non-elite runners.

your stomach. Planning your eating around your running is made easier by the fact that most road races, like nearly all marathons, are held in the morning: assuming that you've had a good dinner in the evening before the race, you won't need to eat much on race-day morning. Your pre-race breakfast won't actually help your performance; but it's equally important that you don't start the race on an empty stomach. I usually have something simple like a glass of fruit juice, followed by a couple of pieces of toast and honey together with a cup of tea, but these should be taken about three hours before the start of the race. If it's warm, it's important to have drunk plenty of water – perhaps as much as 2–3 litres – the previous day, and to have 'topped up' on the morning of the race. Rarely will you end up drinking too much – and if you do, you will simply pee out the excess.

Drinking on the run

In your kit-bag, which will accompany you to the start of your marathon, you should include a carbohydrate sports drink. Starting two hours – and up until thirty minutes – before the start of a marathon, I regularly take small sips of this drink. (Stopping half-an-hour beforehand will give you time to pee out any excess fluid.) I then usually take a final 'top-up' of around 50 ml about five minutes

Manuela Machado, the silver medallist at the 1997 World Championship Marathon in Athens, demonstrates the importance of rehydrating during the race

Grab and run: mid-race refreshment for the leaders in the heat of the 1995 World Championship Marathon

before the start. In this way I ensure that my carbohydrate and fluid reserves are replete on the point of starting my marathon.

During the marathon it is important to drink regularly at the various 'feed' stations along the route. I aim to drink between 100 and 150 ml of fluid every 5 km throughout the race. For this I use a carbohydrate drink such as *High Five Energy Source*, with a dilution of roughly 10 g/100 ml. But whether you drink water or one of the commercial sports drinks, your motto should be: 'Drink little and often.' Don't wait for thirst to arrive – if you do, this is a sign that you are already badly dehydrated. And don't be fooled if your marathon takes place in relatively cool conditions. Obviously, you won't need to drink quite as much as in hot weather, but you will still lose a lot of fluid in covering the distance and drinking on the run is one sure way of improving your chances of keeping going to the finish.

Practice makes perfect

None of the procedures I have described above should be attempted for the first time on race-day itself. You should try out various routines in the course of your build-up and find the one that suits you best. This is especially so when it comes to drinking while on the run. In training this might involve running a looped circuit that allows you to pick up a drinks bottle every 30 minutes. It's even better if you can find a friend to cycle alongside you and pass you drinks at regular intervals. By marathon day, you should have decided exactly what you will eat and drink before and during the race.

Rest and recovery

The harder you train, the greater the stress you place on your body. The greater the stress, the more likely you are to break down with an injury or illness. If you do succumb to a running-related injury, you will start to learn the process of respecting your own body's limitations. This in turn should make you more aware of the importance of rest and recovery in the overall structure of your training.

In the course of preparing for a marathon, your determination to get through the training sometimes makes it hard to sense when you are doing too much. Many runners simply complain of 'feeling tired all the time'. In these moments it becomes even more important to check that you are giving your body time to recover from intense bouts of exercise as well as from the cumulative effects of hard training and high mileage. High levels of stress from training, combined with other stresses in your daily routine, place unusually high demands on your body. If you don't give yourself time to recover from these stresses, the likely result will be breakdown. Put simply, if you want to train harder, you might have to rest harder.

Dietary supplements

Below is a list of some of the *ergogenic aids* (legal substances, commonly accepted to be performance-enhancing) that I use regularly:

Carbohydrate drinks: to replenish glycogen stores during and after training and competition.

Isotonic drinks: to replace important minerals lost (e.g. through sweat) in training and competition – especially useful in hot conditions.

Iron supplements: to ensure adequate iron reserves. Low levels of iron restrict your body's ability to produce haemoglobin, in turn limiting your body's oxygen-carrying capacity.

Vitamin C: taken in tablet form as a supplement to intake of Vitamin C from food, to boost the immune system, thus protecting against illness.

Glutamine: taken in powdered form dissolved in water, may aid process of rebuilding damaged cells in muscles, thus improving rate of recovery and reducing chance of infection after prolonged or intense exercise.

Branched-chain amino acids (e.g. Pripps Energy 2): taken as drink solution, may affect mental agility and perception of fatigue during sustained physical exercise.

Rest as training

Strange as it may seem, rest is a vital ingredient of a good training programme. This is not meant as a 'cop-out'; rather, it is a way of saying that sometimes you will actually benefit more from *not* over-exerting yourself. Consider these various practices.

■ When you are feeling worn-out from training, it may be better to have one or two days of no running. The world's best distance runners sometimes take a day off to rejuvenate themselves, even when it's not prescribed in their training programme.

- If you're unsure whether you're ready to do your next hard session, first see how you feel during your warm-up. It's not too late to decide after 15 minutes of easy running – and if you're still in doubt, play safe and give yourself another day to recover.
- Don't be afraid of doing some of your recovery runs at a snail's pace. It often makes more sense to run slowly when you're tired, rather than to push yourself into a state of long-term fatigue.
- Arrange to do some of your steady runs with a training partner who runs slightly slower than you, if this will prevent you from over-exerting yourself*. Doing this once or twice a week will not lead to a loss of fitness. Indeed, it should make you feel even stronger for your harder workouts.

In addition to changes in your eating patterns, another way of ensuring that you start your marathon with high glycogen levels is by resting for the three to four days leading up to the event. Running training should be kept to a minimum – a couple of easy runs, of 20 minutes each – and where possible you should avoid being on your feet for long periods on the day before the race (for example, walking around pre-race marathon Expo events).

It is equally important that you plan easy weeks into an overall training programme. Plan to take at least one easy week in every six weeks of training – and more regularly if the training is particularly hard. If you are a regular runner, you should think about taking at least one month of minimal training at least once in the year (*see* also Chapter 8, pp. 105–14).

Incorporating rest and recovery into your training programme might also include:

- taking a few days of rest when you pick up a small injury. You will not lose much fitness by having a few days off running. If you're keen enough, you might even be able to maintain fitness during this break from running by switching to some form of low-impact training such as swimming or cycling;
- following a hard training session with a hot shower and stretch, coupled with a cup of tea and a piece of cake, rather than simply crashing out on the sofa as soon as you stagger in exhausted through the door;
- breaking a long car journey to stretch for 5–10 minutes to avoid feeling really stiff when you get to the other end.

Rest means different things to different people. For some, it may mean getting a few more hours of sleep; for others, it may involve putting your feet up for half-an-hour in the middle of the day. For those of you who can only dream of such luxuries, it may simply involve cutting back on your social activities. Whatever your situation, fitting rest into your programme – and thus getting the most out of your running – requires discipline and good organisation. It will also depend on your priorities in life. If something is important enough to you, you will make every effort to make it happen.

*This can also be achieved by wearing a heart-rate monitor during your recovery runs, and ensuring that your heart rate stays below a set limit (e.g. 70–75% of your maximum heart rate).

Key points

Incorporate a healthy diet into your everyday routine.

Pay more attention to eating the right *kind* of food, rather than worrying about how much you are eating.

Make sure that you are drinking plenty, especially when training in warm weather.

Start the process of post-exercise recovery by consuming a snack within an hour of finishing training.

Recognise the importance of rest in your overall pattern of training.

Useful tips

Measures for post-race recovery

To prevent you from suffering too many after-effects of running a marathon – and thus enable you to enjoy your post-race feeling of satisfaction – you should take certain precautions once the race is over. By the time you reach the finish you will have run down many of your normal defences against illness: your body is both short of energy and dehydrated. In addition, your muscles will be sore and in need of repair. So, having crossed the line and got your finishing medal – even if you've sworn never to run another marathon – what should you do next?

Foiled at the finish: Catherina McKiernan stays warm after winning the 1998 London Marathon

In the immediate aftermath of the race, you should:

▨ stay warm – once you stop running, you will lose body heat quickly, so put on a tracksuit or sweat top as soon as you can after finishing;

▨ start replenishing your reserves by drinking plenty and even eating small snacks: the longer you leave it before refuelling, the wearier you will become. Even if you're too tired to think about food or drink so soon after finishing, remember that your body needs desperately to rebuild its energy stores;

▨ try if you can to walk for 10 minutes, rather than collapsing in a heap after reaching the finish. This will go some way to getting rid of the waste products that are likely to cause stiffness and soreness afterwards;

▨ then aim to get into a hot bath as soon as conveniently possible.

In the days following your marathon, the best form of recuperation is rest combined with some light exercise (especially walking) and gentle stretching. Even if you feel that your energy levels have returned to normal, you should resist the temptation of attempting any hard training for at least one week (and preferably longer) after the marathon. This will allow time for your muscle cells and tissues to repair, and thus give you more chance of resuming effective training in the long term. The process of recovery and repair can be helped by having a massage; alternatively, go for a swim or jacuzzi. Continue to eat well.

In the weeks following your marathon, if you still have the urge to run, break yourself back into the routine gradually. After one or two very easy weeks, you can start to capitalise on your post-marathon fitness. But listen to your body and be sensible – this may be a good time to have a longer break from structured training. If you take a good break now, it might mean that you return to your training refreshed both in mind and body.

Table 4.1 outlines some of my post-marathon recovery periods.

Table 4.1 Post-marathon recovery periods

Marathon	Weekly mileage (two weeks post-race)	Resumption of normal training (post-race)	Date of first race post-marathon
Hamburg, May 1993	45 miles 92 miles	2 weeks	6 weeks
San Sebastian, October 1993	67 miles 72 miles	5 weeks	6 weeks
Helsinki, August 1994	72 miiles 100 miles	2 weeks	10 weeks
Atlanta, August 1996	40 miles 65 miles	8 weeks	8 weeks
London, April 1997	6 miles 11 miles	3 weeks	11 weeks

Table 4.2 shows how I recovered and resumed my training after the 1997 London Marathon.

Table 4.2 Recovery and resumption of training after 1997 London Marathon

Weeks 1 and 2			Week 3		
Sunday		Marathon	Sunday		13 miles easy
Monday		Swim and massage	Monday	a.m.	6 miles easy + gym
				p.m.	6 miles easy
Tuesday		20 min jog and massage	Tuesday	a.m.	6 miles easy + strides
				p.m.	6 miles steady
Wednesday	a.m.	30 min jog	Wednesday		13 miles easy + gym
	p.m.	Fly to Crete			
Thursday to following Friday		8-day walking holiday (no running)	Thursday	a.m.	20 x 150 m short hills
				p.m.	6 miles easy
			Friday		9 miles easy + gym
Saturday	a.m.	45 min easy run	Saturday	a.m.	10 miles steady
	p.m.	35 min easy run		p.m.	5 miles easy + strides
Total (week 1) excluding race		6 miles			
Total (week 2)		11 miles	Total (week 3)		88 miles

The European Championships

Course 'recce'

The small Finnish town of Punkalaidun, two hours' drive from Helsinki, was where I started my race preparation for the 1994 European Championship Marathon. It was there, three months before the opening of the championships, that I ran a 5000 m track race prior to starting my marathon build-up. The main reason, however, for my trip to Finland at this stage in my preparation was to enable me to have a look at the Helsinki marathon course.

Following the best tradition of Finnish javelin throwing, the Punkalaidun race organisers had invited Steve Backley to compete at their meeting against some of the top Finnish throwers. Sadly both for the organisers and the local crowd, injury had forced Steve to withdraw at the last moment. Their loss was my gain, as I was offered the courtesy car that had been made available for him! After the race I spent a day in Helsinki and did a couple of runs on the marathon course. A Finnish television company wanted some footage for a preview of the championships and in exchange for a 20-minute interview they offered to drive me round the course. By the end of my short visit, I felt that I had been well looked after by my Finnish friends.

Race rehearsals

After a 25-day period of altitude training at Font Romeu in the French Pyrenees, I finished my hardest block of training for the marathon 3½ weeks before the race and returned home to make final preparations.

The first priority on returning home was to take a few days of easy running to recover from the exertions of previous training. Once I was feeling fresh again, I did my last long run before the marathon. Three weeks to the day before the marathon, I ran 22½ miles over a four-lap course that I had devised on the roads around Marlborough. Each 9 km circuit included a couple of hilly sections, thus replicating the Helsinki marathon course that was also being run over a four-lap course. It also allowed me to practise taking drinks at regular intervals. Bruce and Sue were on hand to arrange the drinks table, refilling my bottles and giving me encouragement during the run.

Over the next couple of weeks I rehearsed a number of aspects of my race-day routine. On days when I was doing hard efforts, for instance, I had an early breakfast and then trained three hours later – just as I would be doing on the morning of the marathon. I also did some more practice of drinking while on the run.

In my final race two weeks before the marathon, at the Great Welsh Run 10 km in Cardiff, I finished a close second behind Paul Evans with a personal best time for 10 km on the road of 28:25. Two days later I flew to Helsinki and went straight to the training camp at Solvalla, a short journey from the Finnish capital, which I had visited previously during my course 'recce' earlier in May. Although Solvalla would be my base for the 12 days leading up to the race, I also planned to spend three nights in the Athletes' Village in the final week before the race.

Scandinavian summer

Training at Solvalla in the warm Scandinavian sunshine allowed me to acclimatise to the conditions that we were likely to experience in the race. Strangely enough, it had been a warm summer in Britain that year; but knowing how changeable the British weather could be, I hadn't wanted to take any chances when making my plans. The further advantage of staying in a training camp was that I was away from the distractions of home, with plenty of time to rest and rehearse my race plans – mentally more than physically. Bruce and Sue were also there to support me. They understood exactly what I was there for and brimmed with excitement about what lay ahead. At the same time we could enjoy relaxing together once the training was over.

Seven days before the men's marathon, the women's marathon took place. This gave me the chance to see the set-up being used for the drinks stations and get a better feel for the course. After the women's marathon I moved into the Athletes' Village as the excitement of starting competition took hold in the British camp.

My last hard effort four days before the race involved 20 minutes of brisk running on part of the marathon circuit. I ran this in my racing kit, at the same time of day as the race would take place. I even warmed up in the same warm-up area that we would be using on the day of the race, to make sure I was familiar with the procedures there. After this run I moved back out to the peace and quiet of Solvalla. My hard training was over. Now it was time to rest, and to build up reserves of strength for the marathon. With three days to go before the race I started my carbo-loading diet.

Carbo-loading before the Helsinki marathon

Thursday lunchtime: pasta meal + bread/jam + carbo drink
Thursday p.m. post-run: bread roll + banana + carbo drink
Thursday dinner: (two bowls of) rice + meat sauce + bread + apple + carbo drink

Friday breakfast: porridge + banana + toast/honey + juice/tea
Friday lunchtime: potatoes/broccoli + tomato sauce + cake + carbo drink
Friday p.m. post-run: High Five energy bar + drink
Friday evening: (large plateful of) pasta + fish sauce + bread + carbo drink

Saturday breakfast: as for Friday
Saturday lunchtime: spaghetti bolognaise + bread + drink
Saturday evening: fish + rice + cake

My weight gain over these three days was around 5 lb (or just over 2 kg). I was already looking forward to my next non-pasta meal! As well as feeling that my fuel tanks were full, I also felt a great sense of readiness to perform: well prepared, well rested, and familiar with my routine for race-day. This still didn't prevent me from feeling nervously excited about the prospect of trying to win the race. But I knew I had done all I could to prepare myself well for competition.

'Let battle commence!'

I came into these championships carrying the mantle of pre-race favourite. My strongest opposition was likely to come from the Spanish and Portuguese runners. In winning the 1993 World Cup Marathon in San Sebastian 10 months previously, I had defeated many of Europe's best marathoners, including Spain's home favourite Diego Garcia. Garcia now came to Helsinki in search of revenge. Unbeknown to me, he had prepared for this race with two other Spanish marathon runners, Martin Fiz and Alberto Juzdado. Together they had devised a strategy to prevent me from repeating my 1993 victory.

My race plan was identical to my winning strategy in San Sebastian. Confident that none of my opponents could run faster than me over shorter distances, I hoped to stay with the leaders until 5 km from home and then make a decisive break to the finish. I also made a deliberate decision not to show at the front of the field until the race's final stages. By following the pace set by the leaders, I hoped to conserve as much mental and physical energy as possible until the point in the race when I needed it most.

From the first kilometre, the German athlete Kurt Stenzel took the lead. The chasing group thought it unlikely that he would figure in the race's later stages so were happy to continue at a relatively modest opening pace. By the end of the first of the four 10 km laps, Stenzel held a 45-second lead. The group then decided to chase him. The pace quickened for the second quarter of the race, and the German was caught at the 17 km point. On the third 10 km lap a number of runners tried in turn to get out in front. I was content to run at a short distance off the pace as long as I could retain 'mental contact' with the leaders. At 26 km I was nine seconds behind the leading group of about 10 runners, and the gap remained the same until 29 km.

At this point the leading group started to split up as the Spaniards initiated another surge. I covered their move so that at 30 km I had moved into sixth place, just three seconds behind the leaders. Another increase in pace ensued, and I moved up to fourth behind the three Spaniards, but still around 15 m off the lead.

But this was as close as I came to the front of the race. With 11 km to go to the finish, the three Spaniards ahead of me gradually started to wind up the pace. Running in tandem, they took it in turns to make the pace, glancing back every so often to see how far I was behind them. Back down the road, and running now on my own, I was unable to match their increase in tempo and started to fall behind. At 32 km I was seven seconds off the lead; by 34 km this gap had grown to 15 seconds; at 36 km it was 24 seconds and rapidly growing. Now it was merely a question of which of the three Spaniards would lift the title. My hopes of a medal were gone.

I had been outrun over the last seven miles of the race by three faster runners. The leaders had run 15:09 for the 5 km to 35 km and Fiz, the eventual winner, had run the next 5 km in 15:20. But I also sensed that I had been outmanoeuvred, since I had never been allowed to get into a position from where I could use my faster finishing speed.

The result was a big disappointment. I had missed the chance to win a major championship title. There hadn't been much wrong with my training or my final preparation, in which a good diet and adequate periods of recovery now played an integral part. I was left questioning my race strategy and what I might do to plan this out as carefully as I did my training.

Spanish celebration: bronze-medallist Alberto Juzdado is greeted by his compatriots Diego Garcia and Martin Fiz at the finish of the 1994 European Championship Marathon

5 Race preparation

Your ability to achieve your marathon goals depends on a number of factors. These include:

- how well you train in the months leading up to the race;
- how good you are at bringing your fitness to a peak in the weeks before the race;
- how well you can get the best out of yourself on race-day.

In the last three chapters I have suggested ways to help you train well in the months leading up to the race. From this you will have realised that the process of good training does not involve flogging yourself to the point of exhaustion every time you go out to exercise, but is rather the result of following a structured programme of hard workouts interspersed with easier runs and adequate recovery. In other words, it is crucial to strike the right balance between effort and stress on the one hand, and rest and recovery on the other.

No matter what your level, this same 'balancing' principle should also guide your pattern of training in the final few weeks before your marathon – the period known as the 'taper'.

Tapering for a marathon

If you were to plot a graph of your weekly training volume over the course of a 12-week build-up, you should end up with a bell-shaped curve with the high point of the curve representing your hardest weeks of training. (Ideally, the curve should be 'skewed' to the left, indicating that your hardest training has occurred in the second half of your build-up.) If you have followed a pattern of hard and easy phases of training, you might even have two or three high points. The 'taper' – or the period in which training volume and intensity are gradually reduced in the run-up to the race – is shown on the graph where the curve 'tapers off' at the right-hand end.

For an example of a race taper, *see* Figure 5.1 which represents my training for the 1997 London Marathon. In your case the training volume is likely to be considerably less, but the overall pattern of high and low points of the curve should be similar.

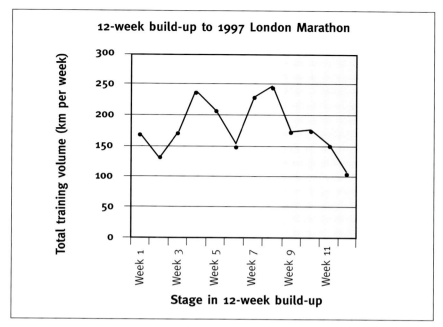

Figure 5.1 Showing a race taper for a 12-week marathon build-up

Emphasis on recovery

If you overdo your training during the taper, you will still have some residual tiredness in your legs when you line up for the start of the marathon. So the emphasis at this stage in your training should be on making sure that you have recovered from all the hard training that has gone before.

There are two fundamental reasons why you need to train less, immediately prior to competition:

- so that you feel fresh and bursting with energy when you stand on the start line of the marathon;
- so that your body is given time to adapt to the stress that the previous load of training has imposed on your system.

Time to adapt

Once you get stuck into the rigours of hard training – and actually start to relish that end-of-day feeling of tiredness – it's sometimes easy to fall into the trap of thinking that you are at your fittest when training at your hardest. The truth is that you will be at your fittest once you have allowed this training to take effect. To allow this to happen you need to allow yourself a period of recovery from the spell of hard training.

Remember that fitness develops from a process of stress followed by recovery. Understanding this principle is an important step towards getting your taper right for your marathon. Only by reducing your training and allowing yourself time to recover will you be able to reach a higher level of readiness to run.

Of course, it's easier said than done. In the days immediately prior to the race, when feelings of apprehension run high, it's easy to feel you ought to be doing more rather than less. Some runners even start to feel sluggish from having reduced their normal amount of training. In these moments of uncertainty you need to restrain any impulses to do more training – and so ensure that you arrive on the start line feeling well rested and ready to produce your big effort there.

Length of taper

How long should this final tapering period last? Though the time may vary according to the severity of the previous period of training, a general rule is that your body requires around two weeks to adapt to the stresses of a given block of training.

I learned this lesson after one particularly hard period of training in Kenya in 1992. This was my first attempt at training three times a day on a regular basis. The end of this two-week period of training marked the start of my taper for competition, two weeks before the World Cross-Country Championships in Boston.

Only when I started to reduce my training did I realise how tired I felt from all my hard training. I found it a struggle to do a run of 30 minutes, when a week earlier I had been putting in over 20 miles of running each day. Fortunately I had just enough time to recover in time for the race, where I finished 15th, my highest finishing position ever in these championships.

Although the race had gone well, the period of training that came after the championships – almost a month after my hard training in Kenya had finished – felt even better. With hindsight it appeared that I needed even longer to recover from my hard training than I had originally expected.

As a rule, you should try to finish your final cycle of hard training at least two weeks and not more than four weeks before the marathon. It's important to balance the need to recover from hard efforts in training with the thought that if you take things too easily in the weeks leading up to the race, you may actually lose fitness. What's more, if you lose touch with the feeling of making a hard effort, the shock of having to run 26 miles on race-day might get the better of you.

Whether it is two or four weeks may also depend on whether you plan to run any races before your marathon. For instance, if you are planning to race in the final few weeks before your marathon, it's probably better to finish your hard training a bit earlier so that you are not too tired going into these races. If you're not planning to race before the marathon, your final period of hard training can finish as little as two weeks before the event.

Table 5.1 shows the different approaches I used prior to my marathons in the period 1994 to 1996.

Table 5.1 Length of taper is often determined by preparation races

Marathon	End of hardest training period (weeks before marathon)	Date of preparation races (weeks before marathon)
Helsinki 1994	3½	2
Korea 1995	3½	2
Gothenburg 1995	5½	5, 4 and 3
Atlanta 1996	2½	6

Of these four races I performed best in Atlanta, when the period of my hardest training finished just 2½ weeks before the race. (Admittedly, my training throughout the entire build-up for Atlanta was superior to the other races.)

Content of the taper

As you taper for the marathon, your training should serve two purposes.

- It should aim to keep your body in a state of readiness for the tough exertions ahead. To do this you have to continue with a reasonable amount of good training, even during the course of the taper.
- While keeping up a certain level of training, you should strive to maintain a state of optimum rest and recovery – especially in the final few days leading up to the race.

To achieve this balance, think of your hard sessions as a means of maintaining rather than developing fitness. Adopt a controlled approach to these sessions and then give yourself more time to recover from them. If you are fresh when you start these sessions, you are more likely to perform well in them. Feeling good about your final workouts before the marathon should in turn boost your confidence about running well on race-day.

The final two weeks before the marathon should be the time when you rehearse the feeling of running at your intended race-pace. Your really long runs will have finished; now, any longer training runs should serve merely as a reminder of what is ahead of you. Resist the temptation of wanting to test out your fitness by attempting, for instance, a 20-mile run one week before your marathon. Some faster running over shorter distances will help give you a good feeling about your running, but there is not enough time for these sessions to have much effect on your fitness. So instead you should think of gathering up all your reserves of energy for the one 26-mile race-day effort ahead of you.

Assuming that you are not planning to race in the three weeks leading up to your marathon, Table 5.2 shows a pattern for your training during the tapering period.

Table 5.2 Training pattern for the taper

Weeks before marathon	Training load (% maximum)	Length of long run	Number of hard sessions	Key session
3	80%	Long (at least 20 miles) + drinks	2	2 x 30 min at race-pace
2	60%	1½ hr	2	3 x 10 min at race-pace
1	40%	1 hr	1	2 x 1 mile at race-pace

Your last session of faster running should take place at least four days before the marathon. Some runners like to do some faster-paced running (such as 8 x 400 m) to produce that feeling of running comfortably at speed. I prefer to run a few repetitions at a more relaxed pace over a longer distance (such as 4 x 2 km) at marathon race-pace. Whatever your preference, you must ensure that this final workout is not too demanding.

In the remaining days before the race you should take things very easily, so that you feel relaxed and well rested. For some, this will mean doing a few easy runs over short distances; for others it might mean taking a few days of complete rest. As well as reducing your training, you should try to minimise your energy expenditure in other areas of your life, especially where this might normally contribute to feelings of tiredness. Your goal is to reach the end of this period feeling fresh and ready for a superhuman show of endurance.

Mental preparation

Though the physical effort of training is reduced in your taper, the final few weeks before the race may be stressful for other reasons. You may have to cope with feelings of growing excitement and/or impatience as your day of reckoning approaches. In these moments you need to reassure yourself that you have done enough training and that your relative inactivity is permitting you to reach a peak of fitness. If you can't do this yourself, maybe a coach, friend or partner can help put your mind at rest.

Visualisation

You may find that your mental preparation runs closely in parallel with the more physical aspects of training. In the course of your training you may be able to imagine yourself running the marathon, staying relaxed and in control, or conversely hanging on with grim determination as fatigue sets in. At its most basic, this is what race visualisation is all about. If you haven't thought about it already in the course of your training, these final few days leading up to a race are a good time to imagine yourself running your marathon and to anticipate the different situations that you are likely to confront as you do so.

- Will you be able to keep yourself from going too fast at an early stage in the race, when you are feeling full of energy?
- How will you react at the halfway stage when you begin to feel some tiredness in your legs?
- How will you cope with running in crowds of other runners?
- What will give you the determination to dig deeper into your mental and physical reserves in those final few miles of the marathon?

The better prepared you are for the situation, the more likely you are to cope when the situation arises. This heightened mental awareness about your upcoming performance should amply make up for the reduced physical stress of training in the final few days before competition.

Key points

Reduce your training and allow adequate recovery in the final few weeks before the race.

Practise running at your intended marathon race-pace – but in a controlled fashion and over relatively short distances.

Anticipate the feelings that you might have to deal with in running your marathon.

Useful tips

Planning a race strategy

Here are some tips for planning out your racing strategy:

- *Start slowly.* Even among experienced runners there is a mistaken view that you should get ahead of your schedule while you are feeling fresh, and then try not to slow down too much in the latter stages of the race. This strategy usually results in a dramatic slowdown in the second half of the race. Good performances are more often achieved either by level-pace running or by 'negative splits' – where the second half of the race is run faster than the first. The point is that if you blow up in a marathon, you can blow up badly and with a long way still to go. Conversely, if you're slightly behind schedule, yet still feeling good, you have plenty of time to catch up.
- *Break the distance down into sections.* The thought of having to cover 26 miles can be a daunting prospect for even the best-trained runner. You might find it easier to break the race down into segments – e.g. in 10 km sections, or 10 miles/halfway/20 miles/finish – and concentrate on each stretch in turn. Reaching the end of each segment will also give you a chance to check your time and monitor your effort, and if need be adjust your pace or time goals.
- *Hold yourself back when you start to feel good.* Perhaps the best bit of advice I received before I ran my first marathon went something like this. 'If you're feeling good at 10 miles, restrain yourself from going any faster. If you're

feeling good at halfway, still hold yourself back. If you're still feeling good at 16 miles, again hold back. At 20 miles you *will* feel tired, and then you can start racing.' The experience of many marathoners is that they hold themselves back early in the race, but then start to feel good at around halfway and run too quickly too soon, thinking that their good feeling will last all the way to the finish. Feelings can be deceptive, however: they then discover that the last six miles of the marathon last much longer than they could ever have imagined.

Start to focus after 16 miles. The same advice as above, but more in terms of your mental focus. It's easy to focus on giving of your best when you're feeling good, but not so easy when you're feeling tired. If you're well prepared, you should be able to cruise along for the first 10 or 12 miles of the marathon with time and energy to savour the atmosphere of the occasion. But as you do this, anticipate that it will get harder, and start to 'focus in' as the race enters its more trying moments and tiredness sets in.

Take advantage of running in a group. Remember that you use up more energy when running at the front of a group. You may be able to control the pace that way, but others have the advantage of being shielded from either wind or air resistance. Running in a group also allows you to concentrate more on your rhythm rather than thinking specifically about how fast you are running. There may be times when it helps you to be at the front, but there will also be times when it is better for you to 'hide' in the group.

Race favourites Liz McColgan (104), Catherina McKiernan (centre, behind 105) and Joyce Chepchumba (101) follow the pace-makers in the early stages of the 1998 London Marathon

Useful tips

Race-day arrangements

A useful way to reduce pre-race anxiety is to ensure that you have made arrangements for your movements on the day of your marathon. The more obvious issues are:

- How will you get to the start?
- Where will you meet up with your friends and supporters after the race?
- How will you get home afterwards?

Nowadays, most organisers of big-city marathons (and the travel agencies who work with them) are highly efficient in putting on services to help runners with such arrangements. However, it is as well that you find out for yourself what is going to happen. Try to be as specific as possible in the detail of these plans, remembering that many other runners will be on the move at the same time with precisely the same objective. On race-day itself, you may be too nervous to think about anything else but running the race, and after the race you will almost certainly be too tired to do anything about it.

You should also be familiar with your race-day routine.

- You'll need to eat breakfast about three hours before the start of the marathon, which will mean eating at around 6.00–6.30 a.m. – since many marathons start around 9.00 a.m. In the week leading up to the race – or ideally, earlier in your preparation before one of your long runs – try out this routine. (For what you should eat, *see* Chapter 4, p. 56.)
- You should have a clear idea of how you will warm up before the marathon. The most important thing is to stay warm before you start running. This might entail a few minutes of easy jogging followed by light stretching in the 15–20 minutes before the race begins. But you should do this without expending any unnecessary energy. The faster your starting speed, the longer you will require to complete an adequate warm-up.
- Immediately after the race, the most important thing is to stay warm, and to start replenishing your energy stores by drinking plenty and even eating small snacks. If possible it's better to walk for 10 minutes after you reach the finish than simply to collapse in a heap. Then, aim to get into a hot bath as soon as is conveniently possible.

Your kit-bag for race-day should include the following.

- Your racing kit. Make sure that you are comfortable with your racing gear by running in it at least once in training before the marathon. Pin your race number on your vest or T-shirt on the evening before the race. If you're unsure whether to wear a singlet or T-shirt in the race, wear both to the start and then decide.
- Your racing shoes. It's better not to race in an entirely new pair of shoes; you should try them out in training at least two or three times before the race, ideally in the course of one of your long runs. Bear in mind that your feet will expand slightly as the race goes on.

- Toilet paper – in case you run out of time to queue for the portaloos before the start of the race.
- Vaseline to smear on your toes/nipples/under your arms/between your thighs – or any part of you that is likely to chafe while running your marathon.
- A plastic bin-liner for a wet day, or a woolly hat and gloves for a cold day – all of which you can dispense with once the gun goes for the start of the race, or as soon as you are moving fast enough to generate heat.
- A change of clothes for after the race – even more important if it is likely to be wet.
- A high-carbohydrate drink which you can sip on the way to the start and as you stand on the start line (*see* also Chapter 4, p. 57), and a small snack for after the race.

You can save yourself a lot of unnecessary worry and nervous energy on race-day if you pay attention to these details before you actually go to the starting line. Good race performances, while never guaranteed, usually follow sound and thorough preparation.

Countdown to Atlanta

Atlanta, August 1996

Sixteen days before the 1996 Olympic Marathon, I flew from my training camp in Colorado to Atlanta, where I was met at the airport by Gail. She had conveniently arranged to do some research at Emory University in Atlanta for the duration of the Games, and was staying at an apartment in Virginia Highlands not far from the Olympic Village.

The evening of my arrival in Atlanta coincided with the Opening Ceremony in the new Olympic Stadium. However, I had decided to stay away from these festivities which lasted long into the night. It was enough excitement just to experience the sultry heat of a summer's evening in Atlanta and to know that my competition was now not far away. The following afternoon I took a further 40-minute flight from Atlanta to join the British team at our holding camp in the northern Florida town of Tallahassee.

Olympic holding camp in Tallahassee

The purpose of the holding camp, on the campus of Florida State University, was to enable British athletes to acclimatise to the hot and humid conditions that we would encounter in Atlanta. The climate in Tallahassee turned out to be even more severe than in Atlanta: going out of the air-conditioned buildings felt – at least for the first few days – like walking into a sauna, with temperatures in the mid-thirties and humidity around 90%.

In the course of the 12 days that I would be spending at the holding camp I had planned to do three hard sessions. I had already reduced my volume of training in the previous week to allow for the exertions involved in travelling. Staying fresh to perform well in my final few workouts was now of greater concern than maintaining a high overall volume of training. My final three workouts were designed primarily to get me used to the exertion of running hard in the heat. Bruce and Sue had joined me, and were able to offer their support during my sustained tempo runs on the dirt trails of the Tallahassee Forest Reserve. It was good to do these sessions out of the public eye, and away from the heat of the action. At this stage, I didn't need to prove my fitness to anybody – it was more a question of getting myself mentally prepared for performing on the big stage in Atlanta.

An outline of my taper for the race in Atlanta is shown in Table 5.3.

Table 5.3 Tapering for the Olympic Marathon (Atlanta, 1996)

Days to go	Hard efforts	Total volume (km)
19	15 km inc. 5 x (2 km fast, 1 km cruise)	3 weeks to go:
16–14	Travel to Atlanta, then to Tallahassee	153 km
11	24 km at good aerobic pace	2 weeks to go:
8	10 km fast, increasing pace	160 km
5	16 km at fast but relaxed pace	In week before
3	Transfer back to Atlanta	marathon: 112 km

Staying in a training camp for the entire period of my taper meant that I had plenty of time to relax once training was over. Indeed, a great sense of anticipation prevailed over the camp as, both individually and as a team of British athletes, we prepared ourselves for competition. Each evening we would gather in the main living room in front of the large-screen TV to follow the progress of other team members who had already started competing. The long hours of waiting filled me both with excitement and apprehension.

In the final week before competition my daily routine of training involved a couple of easy half-hour runs. The total weekly volume of training had been reduced from a maximum of around 240 km in my hardest training period to 112 km in the final week before competition. Now, all my steady running between the hard sessions was done at a relaxed pace. During these runs I would picture myself running on stretches of the course which I had visited three times over the past two years. To sharpen my focus for the race I spent a few sessions discussing possible race scenarios with the team psychologist. I also tried to anticipate the pre-race excitement I would encounter once I moved into the Olympic Village.

We had plenty of time to relax as the race drew near. To kill time and help switch off from thoughts of competition, we took a day trip to the Gulf Coast and had an afternoon at a local resort.

As the Games progressed, athletes started to leave Tallahassee and transfer to the Olympic Village in Atlanta in preparation for competition. Since I was competing on the final day, I was the last athlete to leave the camp. Fortunately, even until the day before I left, I continued to enjoy the support in Tallahassee of my coach, the medical officers and other members of the British Olympic team staff. Three days before my race I flew back to Atlanta and moved into the Olympic Village. The waiting was now almost over.

Ready for the 'off'

The 1996 Olympic Marathon took place on a warm, humid morning (26°C, 76% humidity) in Atlanta on 4th August. The course consisted of a series of hills over the first 10 miles, a relatively flat middle section to 17 miles, a long gradual downhill for the next two miles, followed by three severe rises between 19 and 24 miles before finally dropping back to the finish in the stadium.

A week earlier, Fatima Roba of Ethiopia had won the women's marathon by holding the lead for the entire second half of the race. In the men's race things were likely to be different since the competition at the front of the field was tighter. The tough nature of the course and the conditions also suggested that the outcome of the race would be left until the latter stages.

A few miles into the race, two Polish runners – Leszek Beblo and Grzegorz Gajdus – opened up a small lead. Though they were never more than 50 m clear of the chasing group, they maintained their lead for the next 10 km. At around the 10-mile point, as we turned onto Piedmont Avenue, the chasing pack drew level with the two Polish runners. The pace then slowed for the next few miles, enabling a large group of more than 25 runners to come back together as we passed the halfway mark in 1:07:40. Rounding a U-turn just short of 25 km, the Brazilian Luiz dos Santos initiated a surge. I sensed that after such a slow middle part of the race – over the previous five miles the pace had dropped to 5:15 min/mile, or the equivalent of 2:18 pace – this move could be decisive, so I went with the leading group of five or six runners. But on the downhill section to 30 km, the pace eased again and we were back to a leading group of about 18.

We now approached the series of hills starting at 19 miles. For the past two miles I had been struggling to ward off the feeling of needing to make a 'pit stop', yet knowing that at such a

Running in fifth place in the closing stages of the 1996 Olympic Marathon in Atlanta

crucial part of the race I couldn't afford to stop*. Then, as we started the climb up the first hill, a break was made – and within half a mile the pack of 18 runners was spread out in single file up the road ahead of me.

I tried to respond but was still bothered by the need to empty my system. Then, as I moved from 12th up to 10th by passing Dionisio Ceron and Steve Moneghetti, it all came out on the run! Up at the front, three runners – the South African Josiah Thugwane, the Korean Lee Bong-Ju and the Kenyan Eric Wainana – were contesting the lead. They held a gap of about 20 seconds over Martin Fiz in fourth. Behind them a chase was on for the minor positions.

Relieved of my earlier problems I fought my way back up the field, moving into sixth at the 36 km point and passing the Mexican German Silva to go into fifth just short of 40 km. As I entered the Olympic stadium, the three medallists were entering the home straight. Thugwane took gold, Bong-Ju silver and Wainana bronze, with Fiz finishing in fourth. I was fifth, 63 seconds behind the winner.

*As well as ensuring that I started the race with high stores of glycogen – achieved through the normal process of carbo-loading in the three days before the race – I had also sought to guard against the effects of severe dehydration, a potential hazard in view of the hot race conditions we were likely to encounter. To this end, I drank a lot of fluid – a combination of water and weak concentrations of both isotonic and carbohydrate solutions – in the 48 hours before the race. Then on race-day morning, after an early breakfast at 3.30 a.m. – the race began at 7.00 a.m. – I consumed 1.5 litres of a glycerol drink about two hours before the start. (Glycerol aids water retention in the body, so can be particularly effective where the risk of severe dehydration exists.) Once the race was underway I continued to consume fluids at the drinks stations along the course (roughly 100–150 ml every 5 km). It is possible that after 90 minutes of running, my system was overloaded.

Unable to respond to the decisive move made by the leaders on the first series of hills, I had never got into a position to contest for a medal in the race's closing stages. I was disappointed not to win a medal. But the further I came away from the race, the more I could take comfort in the knowledge that I had peaked at just the right time.

I also realised that the training I had done that year had been right for me at that particular stage of my career. I had trained at my limit and struck a good balance between speed and endurance. At times the training had seemed hard and unrelenting. That I had mastered the task so successfully was due to sound planning, total commitment and not a small dose of good fortune. With a fifth-place finish at the Olympics I knew it had been well worth it.

6 *The race experience*

Peak performance

What is it that makes some runners race better than they train? Or conversely, why do some runners who put so much effort into their training have so little to show for it when it comes to racing?

Your race experience can be quite different from anything you have encountered in training. It's not simply a question of how much effort is involved – indeed, there may be times when you feel that you have to work harder in training than in your races. It has more to do with the mental demands imposed upon you by the race situation.

- How will you cope with your surges of nervous energy?
- Will you be able to exploit the excitement created by the crowds of spectators around you?
- Will you channel your competitive instincts, or let them get the better of you?

If you are able to master these aspects of the race experience, you are more likely to get the best out of yourself once the competition has begun.

In Chapter 5 (pp. 78–79), I gave an account of how Josiah Thugwane became the first black South African ever to win the Olympic Marathon. Thugwane was relatively unknown in the world of marathon running going into the 1996 Olympic Games. Expectations about South African runners performing well in the event lay with his better-known compatriots, Gert Thys and Lawrence Peu, who had already made a name for themselves on the US road-racing circuit. So how was it that Thugwane was able to produce such a stunning run in Atlanta? First, no doubt, because his training had brought him to a peak of physical fitness on race-day. Second, and as important, because he had reserved his best for the race. In his training sessions with Thys and Peu in Albuquerque in the run-up to the Games he had been happy to play the role of the follower. By winning in Atlanta, Thugwane showed that he knew best how to race, and to race at his very best when it mattered most.

'By winning in Atlanta, Thugwane showed that he knew best how to race, and to race at his very best when it mattered most.'

In this chapter I examine three aspects of the race experience that can influence performance:

- adrenaline and excitement;
- crowds;
- commitment.

Amy's story

One year to the day after watching her first marathon, here was Amy – yes, couch-potato, feet-up-on-the-couch-with-a-drink Amy – actually *running* her first one! As she awoke on race-day morning, the butterflies that hadn't left her stomach all week now seemed more active than ever. Her running-friend guru had told her that it was better to head to the start-line with a feeling of dread than one of complacency. So in this respect at least, she comforted herself that her last-minute preparations were going to plan.

Arriving at the start of the race two hours later, she found herself wrestling with a quite different, yet equally overpowering sensation. As she began to notice thousands of other runners converging on the start area, and what seemed like even larger numbers of spectators lining the opening stretch of the marathon route, it suddenly dawned on her that today wasn't only her big moment – it was *the* big moment, the culmination of weeks and months of preparation and anticipation for thousands of other runners and running supporters. She would need to rely solely on her own individual effort to cover the 26 miles ahead of her, but this would happen alongside masses of other runners doing precisely the same thing.

For a brief moment, Amy wished that she could savour – for longer than the 30 minutes that remained before the starting gun would fire – this wonderful feeling of carnival. She was quickly brought back to reality as another flutter of fear danced across her stomach. No, she couldn't wait a moment longer for the race to begin.

The roadside digital clock showed 56 minutes and three seconds as Amy cruised past the 10 km marker. She could hardly believe it: after days of dreading the pain of running a marathon, those opening miles had felt so easy. Amy could almost have admitted to having *enjoyed* running them! Seeing a group of friends cheering and waving excitedly at her four miles into the race had given her a boost, and now – almost four minutes ahead of her schedule – she began to consider abandoning her pre-race plans and concentrating simply on keeping up with the runners around her. After all, she could hardly hear herself breathing so, she figured, she still had bags of energy in reserve.

Three hours into the race, her friends had regrouped at the 30 km mark. Anxiously waiting for a glimpse of Amy coming round the corner, they sensed that she might be in a spot of trouble. Another half-hour later, a weary-looking Amy came into sight, prompting one of her friends to issue a cry as much of relief as of encouragement. This time, Amy did not have the means to respond. Her early surge of enthusiasm had evaporated soon after she reached the 10-mile marker, and for the past 30 minutes of her journey she had felt as if she were running 'on empty'. And there was still a long way to go to the finish. Carried away by the occasion, she had abandoned all her careful planning – and her big moment had crashed.

Adrenaline and excitement

Recognising the different way in which you react to a training and a race situation can help you to perform at your best when it most matters. Some aspects of your race performance – for instance, running efficiently and to a set speed over an extended period – can be practised in training; while others – such as the heightened intensity of nerves before a race and of effort during competition – can be anticipated, but are harder to rehearse.

I learned this lesson the hard way at the time of the 1996 Olympic Marathon (an account of which is given on pp. 77–80 of Chapter 5). In the three months of training leading up to the race I regularly rehearsed the eating and drinking routine that I planned to use for the marathon itself. Despite this, I still encountered problems in the race itself. (For more on the unpredictable elements of competition, see Chapter 11.)

Mindful of the way in which your pre-race nerves might affect you, you should sort out many of the practical details for running your marathon in advance of race-day (see also pp. 75–6). Allow too for the likelihood that on race-day morning, your stomach will be churning more than usual. This might involve bringing forward the time of your pre-race breakfast snack: whereas in the course of normal training you might get away with having breakfast just two hours before setting out on a long run, on the morning before you run your marathon you may need to allow a little longer for your food to digest.

As well as understanding how your state of apprehension might hinder performance, you should also recognise ways in which it can enhance it. When I line up at the start of a race, there is always something that makes me want to fight harder and dig deeper than I am ever able to do in training. Maybe it's because I know that there's nowhere to hide in competition. The race will betray my true level of fitness – I have to 'produce the goods' here. I can still remember that empty feeling as a schoolboy, nervous before some of my earliest cross-country races. Would I be fast enough to get up to the front? Would I be able to hang on when my rivals made a surge? I also used to dread the thought that my laces would snap as I was tying up my shoes before the start (which they sometimes did). Those pre-race nerves felt pretty awful at the time, but no doubt they helped me to run well once the race got underway.

Have you ever tried doing a time-trial in training? I sometimes choose to run a time-trial in preference to a race, because I know that it won't draw on my competitive instincts to the same degree. I want to store up those resources for when it really matters. Although it often feels as if I'm pushing myself as hard in a time-trial as in a race, my times in the time-trial never come out as fast as in the race proper. Why? Because in time-trials I am short of that adrenaline-producing excitement of the race that helps to counteract feelings of tiredness and pain.

Three weeks before competing in the 1997 London Marathon I ran a tough 30 km time-trial on the quiet country roads around my former home in Marlborough, covering the distance in 1:32:18. When it came to the race itself, I ran the first 30 km in 1:30:52 and then kept going for a further 12 km at roughly the same pace. The whole atmosphere of the race occasion spurred me on to greater levels of performance.

Staying in control

If you watch small children running fast, rarely is there a sense of them holding anything in reserve. It is all or nothing; what counts is the present; the finish line is never far away. But while the excitement of young children is unchecked and immediate, the excitement experienced by marathon runners has to be controlled and spread over a long period. If it is not, and too much child-like aggression is shown in the early stages of a race, the runner will soon come to grief. By contrast, the runner who can keep these feelings of aggression under wraps until a point in the race when they are most needed is more likely to be successful at the marathon.

Some years before I ran my first marathon, I remember watching Gelindo Bordin race to victory in the 1990 Boston Marathon. Bordin knew a thing or two about the art of controlled aggression, having come from behind in the final two miles to win the 1988 Olympic Marathon two years earlier. Bordin's Olympic victory had demonstrated the importance of keeping something in reserve for the latter stages of a marathon.

The toughest part of the Boston Marathon course is the stretch of road known as 'Heartbreak Hill' – a series of long gradual rises between 17 and 21 miles. Bordin knew he would have to make his main effort at this point in the race if he were to have any chance of winning. He was content therefore to run some way behind the leading group of Africans in the race's early stages. After 16 miles he was still only in sixth place, almost a minute behind the leaders. As they approached the hills, Bordin started to make his move. By 18 miles he had moved into third with the gap to the leader, Juma Ikangaa reduced to 49 seconds. At 20 miles he was in second, 16 seconds behind Ikangaa. On the final section of Heartbreak Hill, running on the other side of the road to Ikangaa, Bordin swept into the lead.

From that point on, no one doubted that Bordin would end up the winner. (In fact, he went on to win by a huge 93-second margin.) The six Africans who had set the early pace had run the first half of the race in the bewilderingly fast time of 1:02:01. To keep the leaders in his sights – albeit 300 m down the road – Bordin had had to run faster than cool rationale would have suggested. He had covered the first half of the course in 1:02:46. But in refusing to get caught up in the excitement of the race's early stages, and holding back his biggest effort for when it really mattered, Bordin skilfully outplayed and outran his opposition.

Crowds

My first-ever race in the Olympic arena was an unforgettable experience. What made it particularly memorable were the crowds at the Olympic Stadium in Barcelona on that warm summer evening in late July 1992.

We were being called to the start of the first heat of the 10,000 m. A first-eight finish in the heat ensured a place in the final three days later. A few hours earlier, the capacity crowd in the Mont Juig Olympic Stadium had seen their home favourite from Barcelona, Daniel Plaza, win the first gold medal of track and field competition in the 20 km walk. Moments after the gun was fired for the start of our race came an announcement in the stadium that the medal ceremony for

Being seen if not heard: some of my support at the 1992 10,000 m Olympic final in Barcelona

Crowds can inspire you: spectators willing runners on towards the finish of the London Marathon

Plaza's – and Spain's first – gold medal was being postponed until the following evening. The crowd went hysterical in being denied what they had waited all evening for. They started whistling incessantly and waving white handkerchiefs (as a sign of disapproval) – imitating the worst antics of Barcelona's soccer fans. We ran our heat oblivious to the reasons for their hysteria, but could hardly remain unaffected by the excitement generated by the crowds. I ended up finishing third in the race, thus qualifying for the Olympic 10,000 m final. Three days later the atmosphere in the stadium was equally charged as 20 of us – Ethiopian against Kenyan, Spaniard against Moroccan, American against Mexican – lined up for the final where I ended up finishing a disappointing 17th.

Crowds can and do affect your performance. They can inspire you, or conspire against you – or both, as I discovered when running the London Marathon in 1997 (*see* below). They can reassure you, or unsettle you. They can urge you on to an even greater show of effort, or they can make your pace judgement go completely haywire. But one thing is for certain. They won't go away, so it's good to learn to live with them.

Commitment

Getting the best out of yourself on race-day also depends to a large extent on your desire to perform well. If something is really important to you, you will be prepared to put yourself out to make it happen.

I remember once meeting a former Soviet swimming coach from the old communist system who had taken a new job working with the Austrian national swimming team. He complained that though the Austrian swimmers had ability and trained well, they lacked the real desire to succeed. In Russia, he recalled, athletes not only wanted to win, but *needed* to win. It was a matter of priorities.

I have often found that my best performances come after a period of sustained hard training. I know how hard I've worked to reach my level of fitness. I'm desperately keen to demonstrate my true level of fitness. It has become a question of necessity that I turn my fitness into results.

'You should train not simply to get into great shape, but to get into great shape for a specific race on a specific day – and then give of your best. That's what peak performance is all about.'

My coach Bruce had a similar approach in his competitive days. In his races he would expend so much effort in his attempt to drive himself harder towards the finish that he was often physically sick when he got there. The race situation was an intense experience, demanding from the athlete total commitment of effort and resolve.

If you are serious about trying to peak for performance, at whatever level you may be competing, you should try to focus all your efforts on the one task ahead of you. The nearer you get to the race, the narrower becomes your focus. You will need not only to train specifically for the event, but also to think clearly about how you plan to run the race. You should train not simply to get into great shape, but to get into great shape for a specific race on a specific day – and then give of your best. That's what peak performance is all about.

Useful Tips

Anticipating problems on race-day

Assuming that you have trained well, that you have worked out a good race strategy (*see* pp. 73–74), and that you have made thorough pre-race arrangements (*see* pp. 75–76), you should feel confident about achieving your goal as you go to the start of the marathon. However, the true nature of the challenge before you is only just beginning as you actually set about running the race.

How should you anticipate possible dangers along the way?

- *Crowds of participating runners.* You may find that the pace at which you start your marathon is determined by the pace of the runners around you, rather than by your own planned schedule. Don't panic if this happens. Remember that it's much easier to catch up on your schedule if you've started too slowly than to maintain your pace if you've gone out too quickly. You may have done many of your long training runs on your own, but come race-day you may find yourself surrounded by a sea of runners for most of the distance. If you can't physically practise what this will feel like, try to imagine yourself in this situation so that it comes as less of a shock on the day of your marathon.
- *Crowds on the course.* Let them be an encouragement to you, but not to the extent that they make you run too fast too soon. Many runners tell the story of getting carried away by the excitement of the occasion, running ahead of their pre-race schedules and paying for it at the end (*see* Amy's story, p. 82).
- *Highs and lows of the race.* No matter how well you perform, you're likely to experience at least a few dark moments in the race. It may be something physical (such as a stomach problem or a painful blister – *see* below), or simply a feeling of doubt about achieving your goal. It may help to anticipate how you might react in such situations and to develop your own mechanisms for coping with such problems.
- *Being unable to take drinks at the drinks stations* (due perhaps to over-crowding, or a shortage of drinks). Though this is unlikely to occur, you may need to think quickly: ask to share a fellow runner's drink – or else wait until the next water station. (In some marathons, drinks stations offering water and sponges are placed midway between stations offering special glucose drinks.)
- *Physical problems.* Many of these hazards can be eliminated in the course of training (which will have given you experience of addressing such problems). You should be comfortable in your racing shoes and in your racing gear; you should know when and how much to drink; you might even have had to put up with cramp or a side-stitch in training. Use this experience, and the

knowledge that you have endured worse things in training, to help you either avoid or put up with such problems if they do occur in your marathon.

- *'Hitting the wall'*. Technically, the term refers to the act of slowing down dramatically once your glycogen reserves have been exhausted (*see* also pp. 54–57). Once you reach this state, you have to rely exclusively on fat as a source of fuel. This will allow you to keep going but – because of its less efficient work-rate as discussed in Chapter 4 – you will be forced to slow down. There are ways, however, in which you can reduce the likelihood of this happening. The most obvious way in training is by doing long runs which get your body used to drawing on both fat *and* glycogen as a source of fuel – thus conserving those vital glycogen stores for the latter stages of your marathon. (Some runners take this practice to the extreme by doing their long training runs on an empty stomach, believing that when already short of glycogen, the body will become even more efficient at conserving these limited reserves.) The dietary precautions necessary to avoid 'hitting the wall' are outlined in Chapter 4.

Note also that the term 'hitting the wall' is used by many marathon runners more broadly to describe a state of extreme fatigue – whether or not it results in a sudden reduction in running speed. In such a situation, how will you cope? Your energy and adrenaline will be running low. You may experience tiredness either in the form of a cramping sensation or as a feeling of 'heavy legs'. Willpower and determination may be your only hope of getting you to the finish.

On a high for the London Marathon

In the days leading up to my debut appearance in the London Marathon I felt a great sense of anticipation about what I could achieve. The race organisers were keen to have a British winner in the men's race, following three consecutive victories by the Mexican Dionisio Ceron. This year Ceron would not be taking part in the London race, and much of the pre-race 'hype' centred on the confrontation between myself and Paul Evans, who two months after my fifth place finish in Atlanta had won the Chicago Marathon in a time of 2:08:52.

A strong international field had also been assembled. Thugwane, the 1996 Olympic Marathon champion, would be running, but there was some doubt as to whether he could reproduce his Atlanta form. Antonio Pinto, the 1992 London Marathon winner, was coming back to one of his favourite race venues. He had already run four 2:08 marathons, although in my favour was the fact that I had beaten him in all three championship marathons that we had contested. Likewise Steve Moneghetti, the 1994 Commonwealth champion, had four 2:08 clockings to his credit, but I had beaten him in our two most recent encounters, in Gothenburg and Atlanta. Stefano Baldini, the 1996 World Half-Marathon champion, was also in the field, but he was still a relative novice at the full 26-mile distance, with a personal best of 2:11:01. This was a race I felt I could definitely win – if I could produce my best on the day.

Race-day in London

Race-day brought with it near-perfect conditions for marathon running: blue skies and sunshine, and a temperature of around 10°C. As I looked out of our hotel window, the flags on Tower Bridge were hardly fluttering – a sign that the westerly wind that so often buffets the runners on the final four miles of the course might today be a less important factor. We had a light breakfast at 6.00 a.m., were on the bus to the course at 7.15, and arrived at the Elite Athlete tents near the start a little before 8.00. An hour and a half later we were on the start-line and ready to race.

The weather

The ideal conditions for running a marathon are a cool, dry and still day with temperatures in the range of 7–12°C. If it is too warm, you are more likely to encounter problems with dehydration; if it is too cold, your body might need to work harder to run at the required speed. Wind is more a hindrance than a help, because any gains made from running with a tailwind are outweighed by the additional effort needed in having to battle into a headwind. (The same can also be said of the respective ease and severity of running downhill and uphill on an undulating course.)

If you have to run your marathon on a cold day, you should consider starting the race wearing a hat and gloves – which can easily be discarded during the race. If it is too warm, you need to drink greater amounts of fluid both before and during the race. If it is windy, the best advice is to run in a group and take shelter from other runners – but also be prepared to take your share of the lead at certain stages in the race.

Over the preceding eight years of my international career I had had some memorable racing moments. I will never forget, for instance, the experience of racing at the Bislett Games in Oslo, where the excitement of the occasion is heightened by the physical closeness of enthusiastic spectators filling the stadium to capacity. I have a vivid recollection, too, of another race in Norway when I first ran for Britain in the World Cross-Country Championships in Stavangar in 1989. There, the chant of the cheering spectators for the entire 12 km of the race was reminiscent of the incessant 'hop-hop-hop' cries heard on the downhill slalom.

The feeling here on Blackheath Common at the start of the 1997 London Marathon was equally special. There was a sense that everything had come together well for this day. I was healthy and I was in great shape. The months of hard training and the years of waiting to run in this race were over. This was the day to perform. Out on the course ahead of me were thousands of enthusiastic spectators – not to mention the millions watching on television – who would be willing me on towards the finish.

As soon as the race got underway, I tried to find a comfortable rhythm and stay relaxed, aiming to preserve as much energy as possible for the latter stages of the race. During the early miles I was aware of the shouts of encouragement from spectators along the route. Every other shout seemed to be for Eamonn Martin (the 1993 winner), who was up in the leading group for the first five miles, but there was still a lot of support for Paul and myself. Just before reaching the Cutty Sark in Greenwich, we went through 10 km in 29:55, inside world-record schedule (which then stood at 2:06:50).

The appointed pace-makers* for the race were two Portuguese runners, Carlos Patricio and Paulo Catarino. They also had the same manager as a number of the leading runners in the field, including the two South Africans Thugwane and Peu and, more significantly, the Portuguese Pinto. Before the race, there had been some discussion among the runners and race organisers about the time that the pace-makers should aim for at half-distance. I had asked for between 1:03:45 and 1:04:00, while Pinto had requested between 1:03:15 and 1:03:30. Not surprisingly, Pinto's preference won out since it would be 'his' pace-makers who would be doing the running.

The early pace was maintained as we passed through Surrey Docks at nine miles. The leading group was now down to about 10 runners, in file formation: at the front were the two pace-makers, Patricio and Catarino; Pinto followed close behind; then came Evans and myself, Thugwane, his compatriot Lawrence Peu, Moneghetti, the German Stephane Franke and the Spaniard José Garcia. I was still feeling very good, and trying to retain a sense of running well within my capabilities.

The crowds go crazy

As we crossed Tower Bridge at 12½ miles, it felt as if we were hit by a blast of exuberant cheering from spectators on both sides of the road. We were still trying to keep our nervous energy under wraps – though the same could not be said of the crowds. They were going wild with excitement, and for a stretch of about 400 m before we came off the far side of the bridge we were swept along by a wave of encouragement. This was more powerful than anything I had encountered in previous marathons, even including my recent Olympic experience.

*For more information on pace-making and front-running, *see* Chapter 9, pp. 115–118.

Leading the field at 18 miles in the 1997 London Marathon

We reached halfway in 1:03:28, at which point one of the pace-makers, Catarino, dropped out of the race. The other pace-maker, Patricio, stayed in the race for a further two miles, ensuring that the pace was maintained up to 15 miles (reached in 1:12:45). The leading group was now down to eight runners.

As Patricio stepped off the road, I found myself at the front of the field. I then made an error of judgement. Instead of letting another runner set the pace by dropping back to run with the group, I got caught up in the excitement of the occasion and continued to run at the front. After Patricio dropped out, I actually increased the pace from 4:56 for the 15th mile to 4:51 for the 16th mile (which also includes a slight uphill section approaching Canary Wharf). I was feeling strong and in charge of the race and started to sense the crowds urging me on to run even faster.

But this strategy was playing into the hands of my opponents, many of whom – like me – still felt full of running. By front-running I was simply acting as a pace-maker for the other runners, who were still keeping something in reserve for the latter stages. By contrast, I was using up unnecessary energy too early in the race.

After running for about seven or eight minutes out in front, I realised my mistake and dropped back to run level with the group. The pace then slowed over the next five kilometres. We reached 30 km in a time of 1:30:52 (still on schedule to finish in 2:07:50). I was still feeling comfortable – though after 20 miles of fast running my feelings were perhaps not the best measure of exactly how much energy was still left in the tank.

At this point in the race, a leading group of eight (Pinto, Evans, Thugwane, Peu, Moneghetti, Garcia, the Kenyan Eric Kimaiyo and myself) had been joined by the Italian Baldini. Baldini had run a more prudent first part of the race, going through halfway in 1:04:15, some 45 seconds behind the leaders. Soon after he caught up with us he put in a surge to test out how we were all feeling. Thugwane and Kimaiyo went after him; Evans and I followed – though now we were both operating at close to our limit. We regrouped at 32 km and ran together for a further three kilometres. At 35 km Baldini put in another, more sustained surge, which again took Thugwane and Kimaiyo with him. The leading group was now down to three, I was in fourth some 20 m behind, and Evans was a further 20 m back.

This was a critical moment in the race. I knew that if I didn't keep up with the leaders now, my hopes of winning the race would be over. I dug deeper into my reserves and over the next kilometre clawed my way back to the leaders as we approached the cobbled stretch through the Tower of London. By this stage I was doing all I could just to stay up with them. As they maintained their pace over the cobbles, I again fell off the lead.

Survival

With three miles of the race to go, and the feeling that I was using every last drop of energy just to maintain my pace, I now entered the marathon-runner's equivalent of the Death Zone, a mountaineering term for the stretch of the climb above 26,000 feet. I became less aware of my competitors, and even less so of the wildly cheering spectators along the Embankment. I had one focus, and one focus alone: holding everything together to reach the finish line in the shortest possible time. Now it was about survival. If I had had the presence of mind, I could have told myself that all those weeks of training in Tirrenia – the long runs, the punishing 25 km tempo runs, the speed workouts – had not been done for nothing. But this wasn't the time to think rationally. It was more about raw determination. I survived those last few miles simply because I owed it to myself to survive them.

The eventual race-winner, Pinto, came storming past me just before I reached 25 miles. He went on to catch the leading trio, and then to out-sprint Baldini over the final 400 m of the race. His winning time was a new course record of 2:07:55. I finished fifth in 2:08:36. This at least gave me the satisfaction of running 1½ minutes faster than I had ever run before for the marathon, and my new best time was the third-fastest ever by a British runner. Still, I couldn't hide my disappointment. I knew I had tried hard, that I had performed well, and that I had achieved my time goal. But I was also aware that I had failed in my quest to win the race. I had allowed the excitement and expectation of the occasion to cloud my judgement at a key stage in the competition. Had I the chance to run again, I would have done so differently: this had not been my perfect race. Racing, however, is not about what might have happened – it's about what actually does.

7 If things go wrong

The problems of injury and over-training

Have you ever wondered whether getting injured is more a case of bad luck or bad planning? Sometimes – as discussed under 'Unpredictable problems', p. 136 – the cause of the injury is beyond your control. Three weeks before the 1992 Olympic Trials, for instance, I picked up a nasty knee injury when I was knocked over by a youngster charging across from the in-field on to the athletics track where I was doing a hard interval session. On other occasions, however, we run a greater risk of getting injured simply because we fail to act sensibly. We expect too much from our bodies; we give too little thought to where things might go wrong; and we fail or even refuse to heed the warning signs that our bodies are reaching the point of overstrain. (For an example of a runner succumbing to injury in this way, see Tony's story, pp. 95–96.)

Our chances of maintaining injury-free training would be much greater if we were all full-time athletes. Then – in theory, at least – we would have more time to rest and fewer things to worry about outside training. This does not get round the problem that most runners either don't enjoy this luxury, or, if they do, are on occasion prone to act in a manner which – in view of the stresses they are already imposing on their bodies – they will come to regret afterwards. Once, for instance, I gave myself a serious back injury at the end of a hard day's training in the process of changing a flat tyre on my car. Had I acted with less haste and a bit more common sense, I might have avoided the injury.

The reality is that nearly every runner you meet will be able to give you at least one instance where for one reason or another they have succumbed to injury. Yet while injuries may be hard to avoid, some runners have learned better than others how to minimise the risk of breakdown. If you can learn the knack of steering clear of injury, you will enjoy more consistency in your training and competition, and with consistency you will find success.

Monitoring your condition

There are a number of ways in which you can receive information about how well your body is coping with the stresses imposed on it. The most important means, but not always the most reliable, is your own sense of judgement: you should learn to 'listen' to your own body. If you feel an ache or pain that appears to be something more than just tired legs, it may be better to take a few days off rather than run with the problem and make it worse. It's better to be safe than sorry.

A useful way of measuring your state of overall tiredness is to take your resting pulse each morning soon after you have woken up. If it is more than 5–8 beats above normal, you should consider taking things very gently or even having a day off running.

By asking for advice from a coach (or a friend who understands your response to training), you can obtain a more objective assessment of your condition. This can be especially helpful if you are uncertain about either the content or timing of your next training session. Athletes themselves are notoriously bad, for instance, at giving themselves a day off from their set schedule. While you might not notice your increasingly weary looks, hopefully your coach will.

In the case of serious injury, you should have your condition examined by a specialist. Here it can be particularly helpful if you have access to a trusted therapist who can diagnose your problem when it first arises, and then advise you on the best course of treatment.

Support services for the elite

- *Medical screening.* I have found it useful to have regular check-ups with physiotherapists, physiologists and doctors – even when things appear to be going well. Having information relating to my normal level of fitness makes comparisons more meaningful when I might suspect that things are going wrong.
- *Blood testing.* Ever since I started training at altitude, I have had regular blood tests on my return home. I now have information on these values going back over the past 10 years, a useful bank of data for when problems arise.
- *Other support services.* Today, elite athletes are also able to enjoy support from a range of personnel including nutritionists, podiatrists and psychologists. The increasing importance given to these support services is a reminder – even to the amateur runner – that optimum performance depends on more than just the athlete's training workload.

Seeking out good advice remains a fine art, even for the most determined athlete. Throughout my career as an international athlete, I have been helped by the fact that my coach had a good grasp of issues relating to illness and injury arising from his own competitive experience. I have also enjoyed the support of two of Britain's best physiotherapists, Mary Bromiley and Neil Black. On numerous occasions I was able to avoid more serious problems because of their skill in diagnosing and treating my injury.

Mary's remedies for some of my injuries were as amazing as her diagnostic skills. When I had a chronic hamstring problem, for instance, I resorted to running some of my repetitions on the track in the reverse direction to reduce the strain on my weaker outside leg. On another occasion when I was trying to address the same weakness in my right leg, I was advised to wear ankle weights and swim side-stroke in the pool. Within a two-week period I began to see improvements in my condition. Time and again, Mary's advice proved invaluable in getting me back to pain-free running. Both Mary and Bruce have taught me that the best way to recover from an injury is not always to take complete rest. Often, it involves a programme of low-impact training such as cycling or pool running; or a series of strengthening exercises; or some hill walking progressing to light jogging on soft surfaces. These rehabilitation measures also have the advantage of maintaining a degree of fitness while at the same time overcoming the injury.

Coaches and athletes should not underestimate the importance of this kind of support. When things are going well, an athlete's 'support team' may appear superfluous to their immediate needs. However, when things start to go wrong, they often have a crucial role to play. At the same time, as the athlete you need to recognise that good advice is no guarantee against succumbing to injury. Ultimately, you must take responsibility for the way you train and ensure that its toughness is tempered by large doses of common sense. You must spare no effort in your determination to steer clear of injury and illness, the two hazards in running that have been the undoing of many promising athletes.

> *'Ultimately, you must take responsibility for the way you train and ensure that its toughness is tempered by large doses of common sense.'*

Tony's story

Since the beginning of January Tony had been training hard for London. It wasn't easy fitting an 80-mile-a-week training schedule around a demanding job that involved long hours in the office and occasional trips overseas. On weekday mornings he did a 45-minute run before getting to the office by 8.30 a.m.; and his second run was done in the dark when most ordinary folk had their feet up in front of the TV. Tony was not the only one having to make sacrifices. His girlfriend hardly saw anything of him, and was now looking forward to the time after the marathon, when weekends would *not* be spent either training, racing or catching up on lost sleep.

With five weeks to go to the marathon, it looked as though the hard work was beginning to pay off. Despite being in the middle of a hard training period, Tony still found the energy to run two half-marathon races on consecutive weekends without significantly changing his normal training routine. In the first race he ran 1:12:20 and in the second 1:11:04. His goal of improving on his marathon best of 2:28 still seemed within his reach.

With just one more week of hard training before the start of his taper, Tony was beginning to feel the strain. What made matters worse was that at the end of a busy week at work, he had to make a four-hour car journey to get to a family wedding on the following day. On the day after the wedding, he was due to run a relay leg for his club that involved another four-hour drive to get to the race, before returning home at the end of the weekend. Tony was also keen to do his last long run this weekend, and the only time available for this seemed to be on the Saturday morning before the wedding. He would then have to race with tired legs on the Sunday.

Not surprisingly, by Monday Tony was feeling a little worse for wear. On his run on Tuesday, he felt a sharp pain in his hip. By the end of the week, he was in so much pain that he could not even walk without a feeling of pain. It took another three weeks for Tony to get back into his running, by which time the marathon had passed – and with it, Tony's hopes of achieving what he had worked so hard for, for so much of the winter.

Bad luck or bad planning?

Tony's experience is one of those many 'bad luck' stories. But how much was it really a case of bad luck? To what extent could his injury be put down to misjudgement? Clearly it was not a great idea to couple a 20-mile long run with a hard race the following day. Should he not have modified his training plans on a weekend when he would be spending over 10 hours sitting at the wheel of his car? Could he not, for instance, have delayed his long run until the following Tuesday evening – even if this meant one fewer speed sessions with his usual training partners at the club?

Key points

Plan your training sensibly and anticipate where tiredness might affect your ability to train well.
Learn ways of detecting when your body might be in need of a rest.
Take advantage of medical and other specialist services if they are available.
Practise the art of avoiding injury.
Spare no effort in your determination to overcome injury.

Useful tips

The art of avoiding injury

What steps can you take to reduce the risk of injury? How can you become better at detecting signs of over-tiredness? Here are some pointers to help you stay on the right side of injury.

- *Warm up properly*. Before a session of faster running, this should include some easy jogging (to raise your heart rate and body temperature) followed by some gentle stretching, during which you concentrate on the muscle groups that will be put under strain during your workout or race. This process should last a total of 20–30 minutes, at the end of which your body should be feeling warm and your muscles loose. Finally, run a few relaxed strides. By preparing in this way, you are cushioning your body from the shock of moving from rest to exertion, and thus helping it to operate more effectively. You also reduce the risk of getting injured.
- *Warm down adequately*. The above applies here too, only now you also aim to disperse some of the waste products (e.g. the lactic acid) that have accumulated during your exertion. This is achieved by doing 10–15 minutes of easy jogging at the end of your workout or competition. Your muscles contract as they cool down, so some gentle stretching after your warm-down jog will reduce the feeling of post-exercise stiffness.
- *Recognise the importance of rest* in your overall training programme (*see* also Chapter 4, pp. 59–60). You build fitness through a process of stress *and* recovery, stimulus *and* response. Don't try to take short cuts.

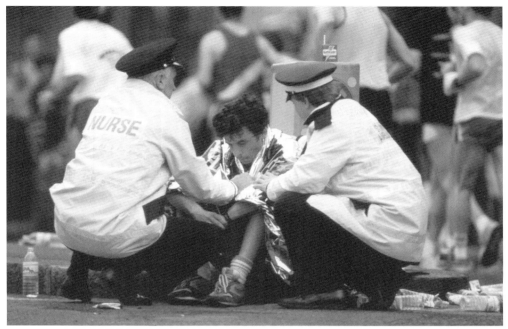
Respect your own limitations

- *Respect your own limitations.* Just because another runner is able to cope with a load of training doesn't necessarily mean that you will be able to, or that it will benefit you to follow the same programme.
- *More is not always better.* More training does not always equate with a higher level of fitness. Sometimes, what you may need first is more time to recover from your last hard workout before you can run your next hard session.
- *Don't play 'catch-up'.* If you do have to miss a few days' training because of an injury, resist the temptation to make up for lost workload by increasing your training load once you are back running.

Useful tips

The art of overcoming injury

The first and most important step towards overcoming an injury is to determine the nature and cause of the problem.

Musculoskeletal causes of injury include:

- muscle weaknesses or loss of flexibility (e.g. calf or hamstring strains). These weaknesses increase the likelihood of postural instability and imbalances between different muscle groups, which in turn can result in problems in other parts of your body (e.g. in the hip and lower back);
- overloading, in the form of prolonged stress or small repetitive stresses (e.g. stress fractures in the lower limbs and feet);
- sudden wrenching or dislocation (such as ankle sprains).

The 'environmental' factors that can influence the chances of injury include:

- running surface or terrain (e.g. Achilles problems and shin splints, which are often associated with running on hard surfaces; sore quads from checking your speed when running downhill);
- inadequate or poorly-fitting shoes (e.g. causing blisters or sore knees);
- insufficient warm-up leading to muscle strains;
- dietary habits (e.g. severe dehydration or glycogen depletion may cause muscle cramps).

Once you have diagnosed your injury – which might involve seeking the advice of a specialist – you are then in a better position to treat it.

Some minor injuries can be treated with self-help remedies. Depending on the nature of the injury, these might involve:

- taking anti-inflammatory tablets or using a cream to subdue the feeling of pain, if soreness persists after training;
- following the first-aid measures known by the acronym RICE (Rest–Ice–Compression–Elevation), to reduce swelling and bruising in the first 48 hours;
- warming the affected area, then following this with some gentle stretching and massage (48 hours after contracting the injury);
- for blisters, draining the fluid, and keeping the area dry and clean – consider also using 'second-skin' plasters. The chance of blistering can be reduced by using vaseline and tape;
- replacing your running shoes if the tread or cushioning is badly worn – usually after 800–1000 miles of running.

Rehabilitation from injury in 1995 involved daily ice-baths for my feet

Many running-related injuries will heal within three to seven days, during which period you will not lose much fitness. It's important that you deal with your injury as soon as it arises, even if this means taking a few days off running: this will better serve your fitness in the long term. Remember also to graduate your return to normal training. Treatment of these and more chronic injuries should also be addressed by following specific muscle-strengthening and stretching routines.

When in doubt about the nature, cause or treatment of an injury, always consult your doctor or sports physiotherapist.

Overcoming injury

As I walked the short distance to the stadium, I glanced back towards the Information Tower that stood in the centre of the Athletes' Village. The temperature gauge read 32°C. Today, Saturday 14th August, was the hottest day yet of the week's competition at the 1995 World Championships in Gothenburg – and within a couple of hours, I would be lining up for the start of the marathon.

Surviving the heat

I didn't lack the confidence to run well in hot conditions. At previous major championships – such as in Split in 1990, in Tokyo in 1991 and in Barcelona in 1992 – I had experienced hot and humid weather and had survived as well as anyone else. I had the recent memory of running a marathon in warm Scandinavian sunshine from the previous year's European Championship Marathon in Helsinki.

The problem more likely to affect my performance on this warm afternoon was of a more fundamental nature. A chronic foot injury that I had first felt during a training trip to Kenya earlier in the year meant that my preparation for this race had been far from perfect. Though I was in good racing shape, my endurance training had been compromised: I had done only two long runs of over two hours in the three months leading up to the marathon.

The hot conditions ensured that the race got off to a slow start. A large group of over 20 runners reached the halfway point in 1:06:52. After 27 km of running, the Brazilian Luiz dos Santos put in a surge which split up the leading pack. Initially I struggled to keep up with the breakaway group, though over the next three kilometres I slowly managed to close the gap and regain contact with the leaders. After another surge from the leaders I again fell off the pace, and soon found myself running in an isolated sixth place some 100 m behind the leaders.

Up at the front, the European champion Martin Fiz was battling it out with the twice London Marathon champion Dionisio Ceron. Fiz eventually came out on top, but only after overturning a 20 m deficit just three miles out from the finish. I ran the last 12 km of the race on my own, gradually falling further behind the leaders. To rub salt into my wounds, a few miles before the finish I was passed by the third of the three Spaniards who had beaten me a year earlier in Helsinki: here they finished first, fifth and sixth. I finished seventh, the second British runner home, behind Peter Whitehead in fourth place.

This had been my toughest marathon yet. I knew I could do better – if only I could sort out the injury that had restricted much of my training in the preparation for the race.

Succumbing to injury

The first hint of a problem had come on my return from a winter training trip to Kenya, when I began to feel some discomfort underneath my right forefoot. The pain grew worse as I trained harder in preparation for a marathon in March of that year. Immediately, I had sought out the advice of my physiotherapist Mary Bromiley. Fearing that I might have a stress fracture, Mary referred me to a specialist for a bone scan the following morning. When nothing showed up on the scan or subsequent MRI, she advised me to run only on soft surfaces until the discomfort disappeared.

A month later I had run my first marathon of the year in a big-city race in South Korea. After 26 miles of pounding on tarmac, my right foot was not surprisingly badly swollen – but I felt confident that a month's break from hard training following the marathon would give me chance to sort out the problem for good.

However, when I resumed training in mid-April, the discomfort in my foot had not abated. This prompted Mary to suggest a period of barefoot running on sand to reactivate the use of the tendons around the swollen area. But the numbing effect of running on frozen sand on a Devon beach in April proved to be more a relief than a cure and I was left searching for another remedy.

Over the next two months I put up with the pain as best I could and resigned myself to feeling discomfort every time my right foot hit the ground. Whenever I tried any really fast running – such as a session of fast 400 m repetitions on grass – the pain became acute. Similarly, whenever I did a long run, my foot became so inflamed that I had to resort to twice-daily ice foot-baths. Even driving my car began to irritate the problem. Meanwhile I continued my search for a cure by consulting with a range of specialists.

At the end of May I had a cortisone injection to reduce the inflammation in my swollen foot. I went back to train at altitude at Font Romeu where for the first 10 days I did all my training in the pool or on an exercise bike. The injection took away the pain and allowed me to complete three weeks of hard training for the remainder of my stay at altitude. I then returned home to test out my fitness.

During July I recorded some good race performances over distances from five to 10 miles, including a 10-mile win in 46:19. The discomfort underneath my right foot was still there, but I was able to control the pain with regular massage and ice baths.

On the day of the championship race in Gothenburg I felt optimistic about my chances of racing well. But optimism can be a poor substitute for the kind of confidence that is built on weeks of consistent, injury-free training.

Overcoming injury

The disappointment of my performance in Gothenburg made me even more determined to find a diagnosis for my injury. Though I had begun to fear that I might have to live with the frustration of running with this irritation, I also knew that without a cure I would have little chance of achieving my goals. To this end I continued to visit a number of specialists in the month following the marathon.

At the start of September 1995 I was discussing my problems with Dieter Baumann, with whom I had trained the previous winter in Kenya. Dieter had himself recovered from a serious foot injury in 1993, so was able to give me the name of the Dutch specialist, Peter Vergouwen, who had treated him. I immediately got on the phone to my friends in Holland who offered to arrange an appointment for me. Within a week I was in his clinic in Utrecht. At last I felt I was starting to make progress towards resolving the problem.

Peter diagnosed the cause of the problem as a bone growth on the lateral side of my big toe, which was forcing the second toe to twist and rub against the third toe. He gave me two options. The first involved stopping running for six weeks to let the inflammation subside, during which time I would do a number of foot exercises as well as continuing with treatment before a further appraisal was made of the situation. The second involved surgery that would require a three-month rehabilitation period comprising six weeks of no running and a further six weeks of gradually reintroducing running training. Before surgery could be performed I would also have to wait two weeks for the inflammation to die down. Since the second option was more radical – and the first appeared to be similar to how I had been treating the problem thus far – I decided to opt for surgery.

When it came to finding a surgeon to carry out the operation, I wasn't short of help. Coming from a family of doctors, my brother-in-law recommended an orthopaedic surgeon with whom he was currently training in Bristol. After an initial consultation, a date was fixed for the operation and the offending bone was removed on 4 October 1995.

Rehabilitation

Then the process of rehabilitation got underway. This involved weeks of running and swimming in the pool, cycling and a programme of strengthening exercises. Over one 10-day period in December, my average daily training consisted of a 1200 m swim, a 60-mile bike ride, 45 minutes of running in the pool, 30 minutes of gym work and some easy walking. I soon began to look forward to the day when I would be back into my normal running training.

I was glad to reach the end of 1995; it had been a frustrating year. For the last three months of the year, during an intensive period of rehabilitation, I had done hardly any running. For a much longer part of the year before this I had lived with the uncertainty of not knowing either the cause of or the cure for my injury. Despite all the help and encouragement I had received, I had started to doubt whether I would ever be able to perform at my best again. Finally, the injury had been diagnosed and eliminated. I could now move on and look ahead with confidence to my next race.

Part 2

Aiming for the top

Cross-country racing in the scenic surrounds of Richmond Park

8 *Periodisation*

A full year's programme

If you are a regular runner, you might aim to complete one marathon each year. The London Marathon in April, or New York in the autumn, may become your main focus for part of your training year.

But once you have run your marathon and enjoyed a well-deserved rest period afterwards, there is still plenty of time in the remaining part of the year for you to enjoy your running and benefit from your fitness.

So how can you get the most out of this period of non-marathon training? Runners adopt different approaches to both training and competition once they have run their marathon. Some like to take advantage of their marathon fitness in the months following, by competing in races over shorter distances. Others prefer to take a break from structured training and are happy to run, either competitively or just for fitness, when time and inclination allow.

It is often the case that you won't know exactly what you will feel like doing until your marathon is behind you. Whatever you choose to do, you may find it helpful to have a plan for the remaining part of the year – even if the plan consists of not following a specific training programme.

Advantages of periodisation

There are several advantages to structuring, or 'periodising', your training in this way.

- It helps you to focus on short-term goals.
- It keeps you motivated.
- It decreases the risk of over-training or burnout.
- It gives you time to work on your weaknesses as well as your strengths.
- It enables you to peak at the right time.

Focusing on short-term goals

Periodising your training will allow you to focus on some short-term goals within given periods of the year.

It is sometimes hard to stay motivated to perform at your best if you go from one race to the next without any clear long-term plan. Breaking up your training year into phases with short-term goals is one way round this problem. Achieving these short-term goals may also act as a spur towards tackling your main long-term goal for the year.

Ringing the changes: cross-country is a great focus for the winter, and track for the summer – on my way to finishing 15th at the 1992 World Championships in Boston (top) and 5th in the 1990 European Championship 10,000 metres (bottom)

During the two years I spent as a student in the States, the focus of my training was determined largely by the seasons of the US running calendar. The cross-country season got going at the end of the summer and lasted through the autumn. Once winter set in we ran indoor track until late February, which was then followed by outdoor track in the spring. Each phase of the year lasted approximately three months, an ideal time to stay motivated and focused on a specific goal at the end of each short season.

When I started to concentrate on marathon running, the other seasons in my training year became less of a priority. I still wanted to be running well in these periods, but I used them more as a means of developing my ability as a marathon runner rather than as an end in itself. This was also partly because the training involved in a marathon build-up was at times so demanding that I couldn't expect to be able to perform with an equal level of commitment at other times of the year.

The other seasons of the year were when I did my background training for the marathon. For example, in a period of cross-country training leading up to the start of a marathon build-up, I would do more hill workouts. Alternatively, if this period came in the early summer I would concentrate on doing some good track workouts before moving back to the road. I enjoyed these phases of non-marathon training because they were times in the year when I put less pressure on myself to be at my peak of fitness.

Staying motivated

Periodising your training will help you stay motivated and excited about your training.

I'm a great believer in variety. At the time of my first marathon in 1993, I was still competing at a high level on the track and country. Following my first marathon in May 1993 I took part in a few track races over the rest of the summer. Then I got back into marathon training for the World Cup race in late October, after which I resumed cross-country training. I loved the variety because it stimulated me in different ways.

Even now, after years of running around the parks near my home, I still find myself exploring paths that I haven't previously run on, and rarely stick to the same route for a particular training session. In the same way, it's also possible to vary the pattern of your training as you go through the year. You can run on different surfaces – road, track or country. You can run different kinds of workouts – tempo runs, speed sessions or hills. At certain times of the year, it may also be beneficial to replace or supplement some of your running training with some cycling or swimming as an alternative way of keeping fit.

Avoiding burnout

Periodising your training can help to recharge your batteries.

Remember that rest is as important as rigour. Just as you can benefit from having a number of days of easy running in the course of a tough month of marathon training, in the same way a low period of training at a given stage in the year can help refresh you in time for another period of focused effort.

Don't lose your speed: short hill reps (top) and track training (bottom) are great ways of improving your speed

Addressing weaknesses

Periodisation gives you the opportunity to concentrate on any specific areas of weakness.

Circuit training or a programme of light weights might not be every runner's idea of fun, yet it can form an important backdrop to your running. When used sensibly, it allows you to work on certain weaknesses that may cause you injury when you are back into a full programme of running training. Common areas of concern among distance runners are the muscles in the trunk and lower back, and the hamstrings, gluteals and quadriceps. (For ideas on how to structure a suitable programme of weights or circuits, *see* pp. 161–162.)

Peaking at the right time

Periodising your training also helps you to retain a sense of purpose as you go through the year.

I have always been motivated by the desire to perform at my best on occasions when it matters most: the challenge has been to raise my game for the one big performance. I find it easier to do this if I've invested a lot of effort, both physically and mentally, during the process of preparation for competition. Structuring your training and racing in such a way that it leads towards such a climax is one way of sharpening your focus on that all-important goal. After all, for the marathon runner there is only one day that really counts.

How does periodisation work?

The aim of a periodisation plan for your training year should be to bring you to the start of your marathon build-up in a reasonable state of fitness – while still feeling fresh and ready for the demands of training ahead of you. So, for instance, if you are planning to run a marathon in the spring, the main part of your build-up will take place in the months of January, February and March. Working back from the start of your build-up, December would be a good time to develop a base of fitness without putting too much pressure on yourself to follow a specific training programme.

The period preceding this at the end of the autumn would be a good time, if you needed it, to have a relatively quiet period of training. This might be the case if you had been racing frequently throughout the summer and early part of the autumn. To vary your training for the rest of the year, you may decide to concentrate on improving your times over shorter distances in the summer, either on the track or the road. Alternatively, you may choose to do some conditioning work by replacing your normal running training with some strength work in the gym (e.g. circuits or weights) – *see* also pp. 161–162.

Table 8.1 is an example of how to periodise your training year. It is geared towards reaching your peak in time to run a marathon in April.

Note, however, that there is no single plan to suit everyone. Work out what best fits around your preferences and your lifestyle. Obviously, if you're a regular runner and have found a pattern of training that has worked well in the past, it

Table 8.1 An example of how to periodise your training year

Timetable	Type of training	Major goal
May/June/ July	Emphasis on faster running over shorter distances. Include some track work	5 km and 10 km races
First half of August	Low period of training	Enjoy a break from the routine of training
Aug/Sep	Increase mileage and use 10 km to 10 M races to build fitness	Half-marathon race
Nov/Dec	Maintain long run, but reduce mileage and include hill work and circuits	Cross-country races
Last 10 days of Dec	Low period of training over Christmas	Recharge your batteries
Jan/Feb/ Mar	Marathon build-up – period of hardest training	April marathon
April/May	Taper for race, reduce training	Race well, then have a good rest

may be best to continue with the same routine. Equally, there may be times when your training will benefit from a change. Adopting a different pattern to your training might stimulate you in new ways and provide a fresh challenge.

Key points

Get the most out of your running by making a training plan for the whole year.

Create stimulus by concentrating on different aspects of training at different times of the year.

Reduce the risk of injury and over-training by giving yourself a rest period at some stage in the year.

Use your long-term plan to keep you focused on your major goals for the year.

Address weak parts of your body by doing some gym work, thus reducing the risk of injury.

Useful tips

Training with the seasons

To the non-runner, running might seem like a monotonous form of exercise. Once you get involved yourself, you soon realise that this need not be the case. You can find variety both in your training workouts and in the distances and surfaces on which you compete. Below are some suggestions for ways in which you can change the emphasis of your training and competition as you go through the year. For details of specific training sessions, you might need more specific advice from a coach; alternatively, refer to a running magazine such as *Runner's World*.

- *Spring/summer.* Speedwork: aim to run some short races over 5 km, on either the track or the road. Alternate workouts of a timed session on a running track (e.g. 400 m/600 m repetitions) and a less structured session (e.g. a fartlek with bursts of faster running) in woods or parkland. Consider reducing the overall volume of your running, substituting it with some other exercise such as cycling.
- *Summer/autumn.* 10 km/10 M racing: aim to improve your best times over these distances. Twice weekly workouts on road or grassland and a longish run (of 10–12 miles). After the summer holidays, this might be a good time to enjoy the company of runners from your local running club and to build up together towards a race.
- *Autumn/winter.* Strength and conditioning: if you're keen to keep up your running, why not try some cross-country races? Include some hill repetitions into your weekly training programme. Alternatively, replace some of your running training with a gym session of circuits, step machine or Nordic ski.
- *Winter/spring.* Marathon preparation: emphasis on endurance (especially the weekly long run). After your marathon, have some time off serious training. One of my favourite ways of taking active rest, for instance, is to go on a walking holiday.

The road to Budapest

In 1997, I learned the hard lesson about training: that more is not always better. As a result of overdoing my training for the 1997 World Championship Marathon in Athens, I was forced to withdraw from the race and was unable to resume normal training for at least two months afterwards. (For a more detailed account of this experiernce *see* Chapter 11, pp. 140–141.) If the answer then was not to train harder, it seemed right to focus on different aspects of my build-up at different times of the year with the aim of bringing myself to a peak at the right time. With this in mind I took a more structured approach to periodising my 1997–98 season – *see* Table 8.2. My goal was to be at my peak for the European Championship Marathon in Budapest in August 1998.

Table 8.2 A more structured approach – periodising to peak for Budapest

Timetable	Phases of the training year
Mid-September to late October	Six weeks of strength work (stabilisation and other exercises for lower back/stomach), hills and threshold runs
Late October to early December	Five weeks of repetition and interval work, with introduction of cross-country races, followed by one easy week
Early December to late January	Seven weeks at altitude: one week easy after arrival, then focus on threshold runs, long reps and short intervals
Late January to late March	Eight weeks with focus on cross-country races, continuing in training with long reps and short intervals
First two weeks of April	Two weeks mid-season break; walking holiday
Mid-April to late May	Start back with six-week programme circuits, building up mileage and introducing long reps on road
June	Start of 12-week specific build-up to marathon; three weeks at altitude: high volume and low intensity, followed by one week easy
July to early August	Race at start of period, recovery, then into hardest training block of high quality marathon-specific work
Early August to 22nd August	Start taper for marathon

The structure of the year

After attempting two marathons in 1997, I decided to run a full cross-country season in the winter of 1997–98. I planned to concentrate on general conditioning work in the autumn, and then to have a good period of hard running training over Christmas and the New Year. My main racing period would take place at the start of February, having set myself a mid-term goal of winning a place on the British team to take part in the World Cross-Country Championships in Morocco at the end of March.

As it turned out, though my training during the winter months appeared to go well, I had some disappointing races in February and March. I only managed to finish ninth in the British Cross-Country Trials and thus failed to win a place on the team for the World Championships. I decided, however, to stick to my overall plan and used the remaining part of March to do a series of road races over 5 km and 10 km, before taking a short break in April.

When I resumed training in the third week of April, there were still over four months to go to the marathon in Budapest. I started to build up my mileage, combining this with some more conditioning work – this would prevent me from doing too much running training in the early phase of the build-up. I planned to run two half-marathons in preparation for the European Championship Marathon. The first, at the end of May, would allow me to test my fitness before I went away to train at altitude. The second, in early July, would be midway through my build-up, and just before the hardest period of training planned for the final seven weeks before the marathon.

Both these races, and the training in the intervening period, went according to plan. I ran 1:03:45 and placed third in the first half-marathon. This was followed by three weeks of good training back at Font Romeu, during which I ran over 290 miles in the final 14-day period. Ten days after leaving altitude, I then ran the second half-marathon, and won the race in a time of 1:03:25. The final phase of my build-up took place at a training camp at Wellington College in July and the early part of August. Here I ran a number of marathon-specific sessions, including long runs of 35–45 km and sustained tempo runs over 20–25 km.

My race in Budapest was the culmination of 10 months of planning, training and competition. Despite one or two disappointments in the course of the year, I had not allowed these to distract me from the year's main focus of being in peak condition for my marathon at the end of August. The period of hardest training had taken place over the summer, in the three months prior to the race. With the help of a sports psychologist I had given careful consideration to my race strategy, and as the race approached I grew in confidence about my readiness to perform.

Race-day in Budapest

After a steady opening few kilometres, a Russian runner went into the lead and opened up a gap of over 50 seconds by the 15 km point. Realising that the leader was increasing his lead, the chasing group of over 20 runners gradually started to increase the tempo. We passed halfway in around 1:07 and at 23 km caught the Russian. We maintained a good pace for the next few miles, which brought us round to the start of the final 10 km lap of the city centre before we headed back to the stadium. Running in the leading group, I was still feeling good but found it hard to assess how much I still had in reserve for the final part of the race. Nevertheless, I decided it was worth attempting to get ahead before we got too close to the finish. At 28 km I made a surge to the front of the field, which quickly reduced the leading group to a pack of seven runners.

Having run the 29th kilometre in 2:58, three Italian runners came past me and took over the lead. The next kilometre, which we covered in 3:00, was the point where I started to struggle to stay up with the leaders. The best I could do now, as I watched the leaders disappear further down the road, was to maintain my position. Running the last five miles in isolation, I entered the stadium in seventh place, was overtaken in the final 300 m, and finished an exhausted and disappointed eighth in 2:14:02.

Reflecting on my level of fitness and the toughness of the opposition, I realised afterwards that my race strategy had been over-ambitious. I consoled myself with the thought that at least I had given my all – in training and competition beforehand, and in the race itself – achieved on the basis of a strategic year-round plan.

9 *Tactics and strategies*

Today's perceived wisdom about how best to run a marathon is to save your biggest effort for the end of the race. Run conservatively for the first half; treat the 20-mile point as 'halfway' in terms of effort; and race over the last six miles.

If you follow this approach, you will have a better chance of maintaining an even pace for the entire 26-mile distance. You might even achieve what few marathon runners are able to do – namely, to run the second half of the marathon faster than the first half, also known as running 'negative splits'. *The Times* athletics reporter, when describing the race tactics that helped me win my debut marathon in Hamburg (*see* pp. 20–23), termed this the 'back-to-front' approach to marathon running.

'Gun-to-tape' or 'back-to-front'?

It is interesting to compare this with the tactics adopted by some of the great marathon runners of 20 or even 40 years ago. It was not unusual then for runners to try to win marathons by outrunning their opposition from the start of the race. Jim Peters in the 1950s, and Ron Hill in the 1960s and 1970s, won a number of their big marathons in this way. Frank Shorter employed a similarly aggressive approach in winning the 1972 Olympic Marathon. His race strategy involved putting in a surge early on in the race and then managing to stay in front until the finish.

Shorter's tactics were designed to give him a psychological as well as a physical advantage over his opponents: defeating the opposition in order to win the race was the only thing that mattered. It was a tough way of running the race because it sometimes meant starting off at a pace that could not be maintained all the way to the finish. It was also unlikely to produce the fastest winning time.

The most recent exponent of this style of 'front-running' a marathon was Steve Jones, who for a short period in 1984–85 held the world-best for the marathon. On the day he set the British record of 2:07:13 in Chicago in October 1985, Jones ran the first half of the race in 1:01:43 and the second half in 1:05:30. Many people have since wondered how fast he might have run had he been more conservative in the first half of the race.

Aside from the advent of mass participation events, the main difference between the marathon races of the 1960s and 1970s and marathon races today is the commercial aspect of competition. At an international marathon in Holland in the early 1950s, Jim Peters' only tangible reward for winning the race was a portion of fine Dutch cheese bought by his accompanying team manager on their journey home – a far cry from the huge financial rewards for winning marathons today.

Nowadays, with large financial bonuses on offer for running fast times as well as for winning races, marathon runners are keen to achieve the best possible finishing time in addition to trying to win the race. Race tactics have changed accordingly; the aggressive approach of Peters and Shorter has been replaced by the more conservative strategy of running most of the race at a level pace and then speeding up towards the finish.

Marathon running in the 1990s

The larger pool of world-class marathon runners today has also led to a change in marathon racing strategy. At many big-city and championship races, the difference in time between the first- and tenth-placed athlete may be as small as a couple of minutes. The increasing depth of competition has meant that the leading runners often stay bunched together for most of the distance, with the fast-finishing winner only emerging in the last few miles – or even few hundred metres – of the race.

Another feature of big-city marathons today is the role played by the pace-makers in the early stages of a race. The practice of using pace-makers as a means of achieving faster finishing times in middle- and long-distance races goes back many years. When Roger Bannister ran the first sub-four-minute mile in 1954, for instance, he was helped by two pace-makers, Chris Brasher and Chris Chataway, for three-quarters of the distance. But only in recent times have they become a regular presence in big international marathon races.

There are two main advantages of having another runner set the pace for you – one physical, the other psychological. The physical one is that due to reduced air resistance, it is easier to maintain a certain pace by running just behind, rather than in front of, another runner. Psychologically, the runner following also benefits from having one less thing to worry about: while the runner in front – or the 'front-runner' – keeps an eye on the stopwatch and modifies the pace accordingly, the runner behind can concentrate simply on running as efficiently as possible.

To what extent does pace-making contravene the notion of athletics as an individual sport? While purists might complain, the only restriction placed on the practice of pace-making by those who set the rules is that the pace-making runner must be officially entered in the same race as the other runners who benefit.

Pace-makers are not, however, officially sanctioned in international championship competition: the contest is purely about winning medals and achieving high finishing places. (The hot conditions in which most major championship marathons are staged further weakens any incentive for the runners to chase fast times.) As a consequence, nearly all championship races are run at a slower pace than their big-city counterparts, with the runners concentrating more on their tactics than on sustaining their optimum pace. In this respect, these races more closely mirror the marathon contests of 20–40 years ago, where the challenge lay as much in outwitting as in outrunning the opposition.

That pace-making has become such a regular feature of distance running at international level does pose problems for the sport. Most athletics enthusiasts watch the sport because of the fascination with man-to-man combat – 'Who is the world's fastest man?' rather than 'How fast can he run?' Not surprisingly, therefore, those races which do not depend on the participation of pace-makers, such as the major international championships, continue to attract the greatest excitement among the sporting public.

Commercial considerations

The status of a big-city marathon depends partly on the number and quality of the top athletes who are taking part. A stronger field of runners is generally more likely to produce faster winning times. In turn, fast times – or even better, a world-best performance – are likely to generate more media interest and enhance the race's chances of attracting better sponsorship in future years. Higher revenue from sponsorship enables the race organisers to invite better runners to the following year's race through the enticement of generous appearance fees – and a cycle of success is set in motion.

Fast times are important to runners because they provide bonus payments from sponsors and race organisers. They also determine the level of appearance money paid to runners when they are invited to their next marathon.

Therefore the desirability of producing fast times, both on the part of race organisers and runners, influences the pattern of many of today's big-city marathons. A pace-maker, or group of pace-makers, known as the 'rabbit(s)' set the pace for the leading contenders. At a set point along the course – often at the halfway stage, but sometimes as far as 18–20 miles into the race – the rabbits retire from the competition, having carried out their pre-assigned task. It is only then that the race to the finish truly begins.

Though the involvement of pace-makers is likely to impose a more predictable pattern on the first half of a marathon, the race's outcome may remain far from certain – even up until the final mile. Sometimes, a runner might try to surprise the opposition by getting clear of the field before the rabbits have finished their job. On other occasions the pace of the leaders might temporarily drop at the point where

Pace-makers: help or hindrance?

Even pace-makers can spring a surprise on the runners they are intended to help. In the 1994 Los Angeles Marathon, the official pace-maker Paul Pilkington took advantage of the other runners' reluctance to follow his pace by maintaining his lead all the way to the finish. Only after crossing the finish line two minutes behind Pilkington did the second-placed Italian athlete discover that he had not won the race – since Pilkington had not dropped out after his official duties were over.

In the 1999 London Marathon the leading contenders similarly decided not to follow the pace-makers. The gamble of the relatively unknown Moroccan Abdelkader El Mouaziz to pursue the rabbits paid off when after 17 miles (where the last of the three rabbits dropped out), El Mouaziz found himself with a lead of almost two minutes over the race favourites. Though the Moroccan slowed down in the final stages of the race, he still managed to reach the finish almost a minute ahead of his fast-finishing opponents.

the rabbits drop out, signalling a 'pause' in the runners' intensity of effort as they gather their strength for the race's final phase. Regardless of what happens in the first 20 miles, the last six miles of the marathon can produce dramatic swings in fortune for the leading runners as the race to the finish unfolds.

Thinking on your feet

No matter how hard and long you ponder all the possible scenarios, you will never be able to anticipate every likely turn in a marathon. So, as well as having a clear racing strategy before you start out, it's also important to be able to work out how best to run your race once the competition is underway. The way you decide to run your race is partly determined by the moves of your opponents, so you must be prepared to think clearly and react while on the run. (For examples of specific race situations, *see* pp. 119–121.)

My first marathon was a big-city one, and my main goal was to run a good time (sub 2:12), rather than to win the race. For the first 16 miles I ran my own race according to a set pace schedule, which meant falling behind the leading group of runners from the race's opening mile. After 16 miles my coach told me that I was rapidly gaining on the leaders who had slowed down from their earlier brisk pace. Then I had to think about conserving my effort as I caught up with them, switching my focus towards trying to win the race. I eventually caught the leaders after 18 miles, ran with them for five miles, and put in a winning surge over the last three miles of the course.

'Racing marathons has been described as a game of "chess on your feet", where one wrong move can prove costly.'

My race strategy for the 1994 European Championship Marathon in Helsinki (*see* pp. 64–67) was based on my earlier two marathon victories. I planned to stay with the leaders until the final two or three miles, at which point I would make my run for home. My Spanish opponents, mindful of how I had won my two previous marathons, were keen to thwart any such ideas I had for this race and made a decisive move to get ahead of me at the 20-mile point. I failed to react to this move and any hopes I had of winning the race, or even a medal, quickly disappeared.

Racing marathons has been described as a game of 'chess on your feet', where one wrong move can prove costly. The art of being able to think and react under the pressure of competition is essential if you have ambitions to win the race. In marathon running, unlike chess, you suffer the consequences of your mistakes both in terms of fatigue and disappointment.

Key points

Run at a level pace, or even with the intention of speeding up over the second half of the course, when aiming for the fastest possible time.
Learn the art of running strongly over the final section of the marathon.
Work out a clear racing strategy.
Anticipate how you would react to the moves of your opponents.
Learn the art of thinking on your feet under the pressure of competition.

Useful tips

What happens next?

Thinking on your feet often involves deciding at what stage in the race you are going to make your run for home. Will you do it after 13 miles, or will you leave it until the final mile of the race? The answer will depend partly on where you see your strengths as a marathon runner – are you a front-runner, or do you have a fast sprint finish? – and partly on how the race develops. Try to imagine yourself in the race situations described below and work out how you might best react.

Situation 1

You are running in the leading group. Suddenly, before you have reached the halfway point, a runner from the group strikes out in front and starts to open up a gap over the chasing group. Do you respond to his move, and if so at what point?

In the 1995 London Marathon, Antonio Pinto made such a move after 12½ miles. Dionisio Ceron, the eventual race-winner, waited for another nine miles before making a serious attempt to catch Pinto. Ceron overtook the fast-tiring Pinto after 25½ miles and went on to win the race. In the 1999 London Marathon, the Moroccan Abdelkader El Mouaziz got clear of the leading group after seven miles and at the 20-mile mark held a two-minute lead. On this occasion it was Pinto who gave chase after 23 miles. Though he closed the gap by almost a minute, the Moroccan still hung on to his lead to win the race.

The halfway time of the chasing group in 1995 was 1:03:30, whereas in 1999 it was 1:04:55. In 1995, therefore, Ceron had no reason to be over-hasty in giving chase: the pace was already fast and it was likely that Pinto would slow down. (This was borne out by Ceron's winning time of 2:08:30.) In 1999, the chasing group ran too conservatively for the first half of the race and thus allowed El Mouaziz to open up an unassailable lead. Even though the Moroccan slowed down in the later stages of the race, he still won it by a sizeable margin.

Situation 2

Just before the halfway point, you open up a lead on a chasing group of runners. After 15 miles you hold a 40-second lead. At this point do you try to extend your lead even further, or do you try to conserve your effort for later while maintaining your lead?

On a humid August day in the 1993 World Championship Marathon in Stuttgart, the Namibian Luketz Swartbooi found himself in just this position after 15 miles of the race. Over the next few miles he further extended his lead by running the next 5 km to 30 km in 15:06, at which point his lead had grown to almost two minutes. But he had misjudged his effort. With five miles of the race to go he started to tire rapidly. His 90-second lead at 22 miles had been reduced to 10 seconds by 25 miles, and going into the last mile of the race he was overtaken by the American Mark Plaatjes. Plaatjes, who had run a more even-paced race, went on to win the title by 15 seconds.

Fast runners, quick thinkers: Mark Plaatjes wins the 1993 World Championship Marathon in Stuttgart (top left); Dionisio Ceron wins London in 1995 (top right); Abel Anton wins the 1997 World Championship Marathon in Athens (bottom left); and Abdelkader El Mouaziz wins London in 1999 (bottom right)

Situation 3

You reach halfway feeling really good. At this point a runner in the leading group hits the front and opens up a lead of 100 m. You are running in the chasing group, and you notice that over the next few miles the 20-second gap between you and the leader remains constant. Are you content to wait for the others to initiate the chase to catch the leader?

In the 1997 World Championship Marathon in Athens, Abel Anton saw his compatriot Fabian Roncero open up such a lead soon after the halfway point. Anton, running alongside his other team-mate Martin Fiz, knew that Fiz would not allow the gap to increase by too much, so he just sat back and waited. Sure enough, Fiz soon started to chase the leader, taking Anton in tow. Fiz and Anton took over the lead after 17 miles. Anton stayed behind Fiz until the final 300 m of the race, at which point he unleashed a devastating sprint finish to win the first of his World Championship titles.

A fast finish in Korea

Working on behalf of the Kyongju Marathon race organisation, Chuck had come to the airport to meet us off our early-evening internal flight from Seoul. It did not sound like an ordinary name for a Korean, but soon we realised that Chuck was no ordinary Korean. He loved things American. He loved the Royal Family. And he was a great fan of track and field athletics, and of marathon running in particular. We asked him where he worked. 'In PL' came the reply. Bruce and I looked at each other for some further clues. Chuck's American English was pretty good, but this expression had us both stumped. Then the penny dropped. Of course, he worked in 'Public Lelations'.

It was March 1995, and we had come to the south-eastern corner of Korea for the Dong-A International Marathon. (Dong-A was the name of the Korean newspaper group sponsoring the race.) Formerly held in the capital Seoul, with all the attendant problems of busy streets, traffic and pollution, the race had been moved a few years previously to Korea's ancient capital Kyongju.

Fast times

My last two marathons in Helsinki and San Sebastian had been championship races. Now I was looking for a race where I could run a fast time. My best time to date was 2:10:03 from the 1993 World Cup Marathon. Now, on a good course and with the right conditions, I felt I could run considerably faster than this.

Korea in March typically enjoys a climate that is ideal for marathon running: cool, dry and still. For the first five days of our stay in Kyongju we experienced precisely this kind of weather. Not only was it good marathon-running weather; it also made for pleasant afternoon sightseeing visits to the many Buddhist temples around the town, as we found our bearings amidst our new surroundings.

The Kyongju race lacked the mass appeal of its London or New York counterparts. In addition to the 60 runners taking part in the elite race, the event attracted only a further four or five hundred other runners. The main interest for the race organisers and sponsors was to produce a high-quality race at the front, with finishing times that ranked favourably against other big-city races. Indeed, the 1994 edition of the race had served this very purpose: Manuel Matias of Portugal (whom I had gone on to beat in the 1994 European Championship Marathon) had outsprinted the Korean home favourite Wan-ki Kim to win in a time of 2:08:33, the fourth-fastest winning time in the world in all marathons run that year.

Course changes

Two days before the race, the international athletes were given a tour of the course. To our dismay we learned that a number of changes had been made to the previous year's course. In 1994 the race had started and finished in the town's athletic stadium. Now, to avoid the problem of congestion at the start of the race, the organisers had moved the start and the finish out on to the street in front of our hotel. But in doing this, they had also changed the route of the two-lap course, which now included three uphill sections. The first, a long drag of around 400 m, came at the 8 km point and was repeated at around 40 km. The second, coming after 12 km, was much more severe, in the form of a hill that rose for over a mile before descending just as steeply for the same distance on the other side. Not ideal for producing fast times! Worse news was in store as race-day approached. Wintry weather was returning to the region, with blustery winds and a fall in temperature forecast for race-day.

At the pre-race meeting of athletes, coaches and managers, the talk was still of aiming to reach halfway in around 1:04:00 for a finishing time inside the existing course record. The pace for the first half of the race would be set by the Polish runner Wieslaw Perszke. I knew Perszke well from training-camp days at Font Romeu. He took a strictly commercial attitude towards his sport: to do well in running meant earning as much money as possible. Here, his pay cheque would come on the condition that as the designated rabbit he ran to time for the first half of the race.

Race-day in Korea

As forecast, Sunday 19th March 1995 turned out to be a cold (5°C) and windy morning. The race got underway at 9.00 a.m., with about 15 leading international runners settling in behind the pace-maker. Negotiating the first uphill section without any problems, we passed the 10 km point in 30:23 – on schedule to run around 2:08:00 – and then we headed out towards the second, larger loop beyond the town limits.

As we approached the second hilly section of the course at 12 km, our pace-maker Perszke suddenly stepped off the road unable to keep to pace. As a result we were left to make the pace ourselves. The tempo inevitably slowed as we ascended the long climb ahead of us. Although we accelerated down the other side, we were well behind schedule at the halfway point (reached in just outside 1:05:00).

At this point we turned into the most exposed part of the course and the pace slowed even more, with none of the runners in the leading group willing to take it up. We covered the 10 km from 20 km to 30 km in 32:24 (slower than 2:16 pace). As we approached the last six miles of the race the leading group still comprised about 12 runners.

Race to the finish

Knowing that big-city marathons often boil down to running fast for the first 20 miles and racing hard for the last six, my pre-race strategy had included an option of making a winning break at around the 32–34 km mark. In the week leading up to the event, I had done some fast running on this stretch of the course as a form of race rehearsal.

The slower-than-expected pace for the first 20 miles of the race necessitated a change in race strategy. A run for home from six miles out with a dozen good runners on my shoulder would be a risky business. I decided to wait until around 35–37 km before trying to strike out for the finish.

At 34 km the local favourite Lee Bong-Ju (who went on to win the silver medal in the 1996 Atlanta Olympic Marathon) made a sudden surge to run ahead of the chasing group. Together with the Mexican runner Andres Espinosa, I immediately set off to catch him. One kilometre up the road we were back on the Korean's heels, at which moment Bong-Ju again accelerated and opened up a small gap. Espinosa and myself tried desperately to hang on. On the approach to the last hill at 40 km, the Korean finally saw us off with another race-winning surge. I was left to battle it out for second place, which I snatched from the Mexican in the final 200 m of the race.

The fastest section of the race had been the last five miles, with the Korean running a 5 km split to 40 km of 15:05. The Korean's winning time was 2:10:58, I ran 2:11:03, and Espinosa 2:11:08. As the pace increased in the latter stages of the race, I had hung on well and was pleased to take second place. But it was disappointing that the race had not given us the opportunity to run at our fastest. The weather, the course and the pace-making had failed to live up to our expectations.

Nevertheless, Chuck was suitably impressed. And even more so when, during the long wait for urine in the post-race drug-test, Bruce mentioned to him how loyal a wife Sue was. 'Aahhh, holy cow,' gasped Chuck, 'you mean, member of Loyal Family?'

10 *The full-time athlete*

For most people, running is and will always remain a leisure activity. Though it demands great effort and fills you with ambition, it still remains a hobby, something you pursue to varying degrees of commitment purely for the love of it.

At the elite level, running is no longer a sport practised by amateurs. Gone are the days of Dave Bedford and Brendan Foster, heroes from my childhood days, when an athlete's training was fitted in around a normal day's work. Today's elite athletes are full-time professionals in their sport. Their whole lifestyle is geared around their training and competitive needs.

Running as a way of life

The process of devoting oneself single-mindedly to training and competition is enhanced when runners come together to live in a training-camp environment. The camp provides both for their training needs – the support of training partners and coaches – and for their needs outside training, such as meals, accommodation and medical support. In such an environment, away from the distractions of home and family life, athletes are able to focus on the task at hand: the continual daily cycle of training and recovery.

During my career as a full-time athlete I have regularly experienced the rhythm of training-camp life. At the Italian National Olympic Training Centre in Tirrenia, near Pisa, for instance, I often got the feeling that a day involving nothing other than training, eating and relaxing was a perfectly normal way to live. This is how our day was structured:

- an early-morning breakfast would be followed by a strong coffee over the morning's sports newspapers;
- training got underway at around 10.30 and lasted until lunchtime;
- after a good helping of Italian pasta and salad, we were ready for our afternoon siesta;
- in the late afternoon we went into town for a quick espresso before returning for a second, lighter load of training;
- gym work, jacuzzi and massage were fitted in before another good meal in the evening.

A privilege of the elite?

The good news for the amateur runner is that the benefits of training-camp life can be enjoyed by everyone – whatever your level of running. Though you might not have the time or money to indulge in your training to quite the same extent as the full-time professional, this need not mean that you totally miss out on the experience. You can organise to spend a weekend away with other runners and get in on the act. It might even give you that extra spring in your stride for when you return to your normal routine.

Benefits of training-camp life

Some of the benefits that I have experienced from spending time in training-camp environments include:

- the company of training partners;
- training in warm weather and at altitude;
- more time to rest and recover;
- access to coaching and medical support;
- the opportunity to learn from others;
- increased confidence and purpose about training.

Training with others in the Algarve sunshine

1993 London Marathon winner Eamonn Martin training in Lanzarote in 1994

Getting involved

I first started going to training camps at the age of 12. Each year our school cross-country club held a pre-season training camp on a farm field just outside the village of Westwell in Kent. The camp lasted a week, comprising four days of twice-daily training and a day out in Margate, followed by an end-of-week relay on the Saturday before we travelled back home. Often, there were as many as 50 boys attending. We were divided up into teams to carry out campsite duties on a rota basis. Between training we ate and slept, played football during the day and – age permitting – went to the pub in the evening. It was a great way to get back into the routine of training at the end of the summer holidays.

I soon made it a habit to enjoy the fun and stimulation of going away on training camps. During my time at university, we used to organise pre-season and mid-season camps in the New Forest and at Featherstone Castle in Northumbria. When I spent a year studying in Russia, I went away to a training camp in the Caucasus in the refreshingly named spa town of Mineral Waters. At the end of my first year of study in the States, I spent three weeks training in Vancouver on the West Coast of Canada before returning to Britain to run in the 1988 Olympic Trials.

Training-camp life, as I was then experiencing it, centred on the enjoyment of being away with friends and travelling to new places. In my school and college days, running camp was about training and living together with other members of the club as we targeted our efforts towards a common goal. The places I travelled to in Russia and Canada enjoyed an ideal climate for distance running. I also appreciated the opportunity to learn from the other athletes and coaches with whom I was training. Our coach in Russia, for instance, was Nikolai Sviridov who had placed fifth in the 1972 Olympic 10,000 metres. In Canada I trained with two Canadian Olympians, Peter Butler and Paul Williams. Already at this early stage, these aspects of training-camp life started to play a big motivating role in my running – and would continue to do so for many years to come.

Altitude and warm-weather

When I moved to Marlborough in the summer of 1989, Bruce was keen for me to experiment with training at altitude. The use of altitude training as a means of boosting the oxygen-carrying capacity of distance-runners had been commonly practised around the time of the 1968 Olympic Games in Mexico City. But through the 1970s and 1980s, it had fallen out of fashion among the majority of the world's best runners. Bruce himself had taken part in some trials to test the benefits of altitude training during his own competitive career in the late 1960s, and had followed this with two years in Kenya in the early 1970s where he had worked as a coach to some of Kenya's top runners. Now, in the late 1980s, the Kenyans were beginning to emerge as the dominant force in the world of distance running. Besides, at that time the world-record holder at 10,000 metres, Arturo Barrios of Mexico, and at the marathon, Belayneh Dinsamo of Ethiopia, both lived and trained at altitude. It seemed to be a case of, 'If you want to beat them, join them.'

In early December 1989 we were on a plane to Kenya, leaving behind us the cold of the British winter. It was a welcome change to be training in vest and shorts in the warm African sunshine, and such a boost to my winter's training. I caught the bug and never looked back. Over the following nine years I regularly went back to Kenya for training, nearly always over the Christmas period to escape the worst weather of the British winter.

For the first three or four years our training base was the Naro Moru River Lodge, on the western edge of Mount Kenya, at an altitude of 6400 feet. Together with Bruce and Sue and a group of training partners from home, we lived in self-catering cottages. We would train on the foot-slopes leading up the mountain as well as on the plains extending west to the Aberdare Hills. (Rarely would we get chance to train with Kenyan runners, since at this time most of them trained either in army camps around Nairobi, or at their homes in the Eldoret region in the western part of the country.) We were surrounded by stunningly beautiful scenery. We enjoyed days of unbroken sunshine. We also warmed to the friendliness of local people and the encouragement of interested onlookers, not to mention the spontaneous involvement of excited youngsters.

On one training stay in Kenya in February 1992, I spent three days at the Kenyan National Training Camp, which was being held at St Mark's Teacher Training College near Embu. As expected, the training regime was tough; yet, in the environment of other motivated athletes, I rose eagerly to the challenge. On several days we did three training runs. On the so-called 'rest day' – it included only *one* training session! – we got up shortly before six, were driven by bus 12 miles down the hillside, and then told to run back through the coffee plantations to the camp. On returning to the camp, I was told: 'Today we must rest, because

Font Romeu in the Pyrenees, Paula Radcliffe's favourite training venue, has also become her second home.

tomorrow will be very hard.' So rest I did, as another day of 25 miles of running (including some tough hill climbs) lay ahead.

There was an overriding sense of doing the training together and helping each other get through the programme. I was frequently exhorted to eat more *ugali* (a common Kenyan dish made from maize-meal) 'because tomorrow we need to be very strong'. Here too, the group dynamic was central to the success of the training.

Life in a training centre

While Kenya fast became my favourite winter training location, during the European summer from 1991 onwards we regularly went to train at altitude in Font Romeu, a French National Training Centre in the eastern Pyrenees. The great advantage of Font Romeu lay in the fact that the centre is a purpose-built multi-sport complex. Athletes live and train on-site, with meals provided. Situated at an altitude of 6000 feet, the centre houses a tartan running track, several gymnasia, swimming pools, jacuzzi and sauna rooms, and good medical facilities. It is surrounded by miles of scenic running trails. Typically in the summer, the sun shines all day long; yet the cool, dry mountain air ensures near-perfect running conditions.

During my stays in Font Romeu I usually trained harder than I did at home, yet the training took place in an environment where all my other needs – in the form of meals, rest and recuperation – were taken care of. I was also away from the distractions of home and able to concentrate on the business of training, and recovering from training. Besides the specific training benefits, there was also the

Training in Embu with the Kenyans in 1992 (John Ngugi is on far left, Paul Tergat on far right)

fun and stimulation of living in the presence of other highly motivated athletes, with whom I trained and relaxed after the training was done. As the years went by, I developed many friendships with other international athletes whom I met at Font Romeu.

Learning from others

Looking back over training camps I have enjoyed in recent years, I can recall many instances where I have benefited from sharing knowledge with other athletes and coaches. I have picked up ideas on altitude training from José Marin, a former athlete and now Spanish race-walking coach. I have observed the training regime practised by the group of Mexican distance runners under the supervision of the well-known marathon coach Rodolfo Gomez; and have trained alongside Australia's marathon legend, Steve Moneghetti. I have discussed ideas with many of Italy's top distance-running coaches, including Luciano Gigliotti who coached the 1988 Olympic Marathon champion Gelindo Bordin. I also learned some new methods of marathon training from Dieter Hogan, coach and partner to the three-time Boston Marathon winner Uta Pippig. In short, training camps have provided a great opportunity to learn from and share ideas with others.

Training camps offer more than shared experiences of training. They also give you an insight into the lifestyle of other runners and the approach they take to their sport. In this respect Dieter Baumann, the 1992 Olympic 5000 m champion, has been one of my role models for learning how to get the best out of yourself. On camps where we trained together, both in Kenya and in Europe, it became apparent how focused Dieter was on getting the most out of every training session. An easy recovery run was approached with the same seriousness as a hard

Top performer: Dieter Baumann at his best when winning
the 1992 Olympic 5000 metres

workout: every session had a purpose in the overall plan. Dieter is a great performer – both on and off the track – when it comes to the big occasion. No doubt this explains why his training, though a vital part of his preparation, always remained one step removed from what his sport was really about – namely, the cut and thrust of competition. These were qualities that I wanted to make my own. It was fun spending time with Dieter. And some of his motivation to succeed also rubbed off on me.

'I train, therefore I am'

Throughout my international career, I have often gained a clearer sense of purpose about my training by going away to a training camp. When I stayed at home I could train well, but there were always other things that demanded my attention. When I was away at a training camp, my sole reason for being there was to train. To this end, I often scheduled periods away in training camps during the most important phase of a build-up to a major race. It invariably happened also that my increased focus on training while away in a camp fed my confidence as I prepared for competition.

Training camps are both good for your health and good for fitness. If you're lucky or resourceful enough to get a taste of training-camp life for yourself, I'm sure it will give your running a boost and only make you hanker for more.

Useful tips

Putting your running first

Have you ever wanted to get really serious about your running? Not to have to
compromise your training at every turn because of other commitments in your
life? Well, just maybe, running a marathon might be the time to break out of your
normal, hectic stream of activities and indulge in a more running-centred
approach to life. Whether you're running your marathon as a once-in-a-lifetime
experience or having a second or third crack at it, your heightened focus on
running need only last for the two to three months leading up to your marathon.
I'm sure you won't regret it!

Not all of you will be in a position to take up each of the suggestions that
follow, but I hope there's at least something that might grab your fancy and
become a reality for you in the midst of your otherwise busy lives. After all, where
there's a will . . .

- *Be a full-time athlete for a day*. Arrange a workout with a group of running
  friends. Finish your session at a sports centre where you have time to stretch
  properly at the end of a hard session. Even better, jump in the pool for 10
  minutes to relax those weary muscles. Refuel as you go with a bagel, banana
  and fruit juice. After a proper meal back home, have a lie-down to speed the
  process of recovery – for today, the shopping/ironing/cooking/cleaning can
  wait a while longer. Once in a while, arrange to have a massage or see a
  physiotherapist to check that you remain in good working order.
- *Be a full-time athlete for a weekend*. Your business associate has golfing
  weekends away, your best friend goes off to music festivals, and your kids
  have sleepovers – but you've never yet experienced a weekend given over
  exclusively to training. If you can't find them advertised in the running
  magazines, then create your own. All you need are a few training partners, a
  venue with plenty of good off-road running, and a comfortable place to relax
  over some good food.
- *Be a full-time athlete for a week*. The ideal option is a week away on a training
  camp with other runners in the Algarve or on Lanzarote (as regularly
  advertised in the monthly running magazines). Here you'll meet up with
  others who share your enthusiasm for training. You'll also be able to pick the
  brains of more experienced runners and coaches who are on hand to pass on
  advice. The low-cost, stay-at-home substitute involves using your week's
  holiday from work to enjoy more time to rest after your hard training
  sessions. Take advantage of your free time to have a massage or sauna. Make
  sure your training – including time for refreshment and relaxation – is
  finished before you attend to other matters.

Training camp in Kenya

Nyahururu, December 1998

My first exposure to Kenyan training camps was in 1992, when I attended the National Team camp prior to the 1992 World Cross-Country Championships. That was back in the days when Ngugi still reigned supreme on the country, William Sigei had yet to emerge as a future 10,000 m world-record holder, and the softly spoken Paul Tergat had not yet competed outside Kenya (although in 1992 he had just won his first national title at the Kenyan Cross-Country Championships).

Over many winters since then, I have enjoyed training with Kenyan runners on their home soil in warm African sunshine. Though some of the names and faces of the emerging stars of Kenyan distance-running change from one year to the next, what seldom seems to change is the athletes' determination to make it to the top. If anything, their desire to suceed only seems to increase as the competition gets fiercer.

The Central Highlands of Kenya in early December enjoys a great climate for runners. As our training camp in Nyahururu (at 7800 feet and 150 miles north of Nairobi) is only two miles from the equator, a day in winter is the same as in summer: the sun rises shortly after 6.00 a.m. and sets shortly after 6.00 p.m. Midday temperatures peak at around 25°C.

December 1998 finds me in the company of over 50 international-level runners from 800 m to the marathon, who are disciplined and motivated to train hard. At the same time, they are welcoming to outsiders and sociable when it comes to relaxing in the sunshine after training. Our diet is simple yet nutritious: toast and jam for breakfast; beef or vegetable stew with rice for lunch; *ugali* and chicken for dinner. Snacks between meals come in the form of fruit or grilled corn-on-the-cob. Kenyan *chai* (drunk with hot milk and spoonfuls of sugar) always does a good job of refreshing weary athletes.

Training with the Kenyans in Nyahururu in 1998

The less appealing aspects of training-camp life start with the 5.45 a.m. alarm for the first morning run at 6.00. Though we enjoy 12 hours of unbroken sunshine each day, it's still dark as we start our run in tracksuits, and sometimes even hats and gloves. Our next problem crops up when we're back from our run and discover that there's no water in the hotel. This means having to wash ourselves down from a tub of cold water, clean our teeth from bottled water and leave the washing of our dirty shorts and socks until the supply has returned. Then it's down for tea and toast in the restaurant. This brightens us up for a while, but we're still a little tired when the second morning run comes around at 10.00 a.m.

Kenyan athletes have the knack of helping each other get through a day's training. It's what I call 'the *sukumawiki* effect': *sukumawiki* literally means 'push the week forwards' and happens to be the Swahili name for a favourite athletes' meal of spinach stew. For every complaint of tiredness comes in equal measure an encouragement to keep up and stay the course.

Once we reach lunchtime the day's training is over, and we have all afternoon and evening to recover. The Kenyan secret to being able to train hard is simply to allow yourself time to rest hard after the training.

Our regular routine is a 6.00 a.m. run (of between 40 and 60 minutes), followed by a second morning session at 10.00 (sometimes a hill workout, or a track session, or some sprint drills on the sports field). Sometimes we just do one (slightly longer) early morning run and get into resting mode straight after our 8.00 a.m. breakfast.

By midday it's getting quite hot, and we amble up into town to a local restaurant for a hot lunch of *ugali* and beef stew. Then it's back to the hotel for a long afternoon rest. As dusk approaches, we start to think ahead to our next workout as word spreads round the camp about the following morning's training . . .

One Thursday morning this involved a 50-minute early morning run, followed at 10.00 a.m. by a 4 km time-trial. This was the start of a long selection process that culminates each year in late February when the Kenyan teams for the World Cross-Country Championships are finally decided. On this occasion I finished a minute behind former world cross-country silver medallist Paul Koech, yet Paul himself only managed third behind James Koskei, one of Kenya's emerging young talents.

On the same day, 50 miles to the east in Nanyuki where the Kenyan Air Force has a base, a 12 km time-trial was won by Benjamin Limo (who went on to win the 1999 World Short-Cross title). Ismail Kirui placed sixth and Joseph Keter, the 1996 Olympic 3000 m steeplechase champion, 10th. A fortnight earlier in Nairobi, at the Kahawa Barracks Trials, the winner had been Simon Maino, the 1998 Commonwealth 10,000 m champion.

If I ever needed one, here was another reminder of the wealth of talent in Kenyan distance-running. While what seem like swarms of Kenyan distance-runners race on the track and country each year in Europe, there are even greater swarms still back in Kenya competing to get on the next plane out of Nairobi.

11 *Picking up the pieces*

In the introduction to this book I asked what it took to run a marathon. The most basic requirement, I suggested, was a commitment of effort and determination to get you through the training and round the 26-mile distance. If you're prepared to make that commitment, then you should consider yourself capable of completing a marathon – regardless of athletic talent or proven running ability.

A brief summary

My advice in the early chapters of this book was based on this premise. Apply yourself seriously to your training and make a wholehearted effort to get the most out of your running, and you will be rewarded with a fulfilling marathon experience. Sound planning (Chapter 2), followed by methodical, race-specific training (Chapter 3) sustained by a good diet and sufficient recovery periods (Chapters 4 and 5), should form the basis of your preparation. Couple this with a determination to avoid illness and injury, and the right mental approach to competition (Chapters 6 and 7), and you should have every chance of completing your marathon successfully.

If you are a regular runner, you will have higher ambitions for your marathon. You will be interested not just in completing your event, but also in running a *good* one. In other words, you will be hoping to achieve a particular time goal for the race. The second half of this book is written with these higher goals in mind. You may want to take a more serious approach to planning out your training for the whole year (Chapter 8). Considering ways of improving your racing strategy (Chapter 9) and making running more of a priority in your life (Chapter 10) may also contribute to better performances in your running.

At whatever level you aspire to compete, one thing should have become clear in the course of reading this book: *the marathon is a tough event.* Even assuming that your training and race experiences turn out well, your powers of endurance will be stretched to the limit as you learn to cope with high levels of fatigue and discomfort. But, as I pointed out in the book's introduction, the marathon presents other hazards that can be equally demanding: compared to other distance races, there are so many more things that can go wrong in the marathon.

In this last short section, I want to consider where some of these problems might arise. Some are potentially avoidable, given careful planning and preparation. Others are simply beyond human control – and then it is how you *respond* to the problem that marks you out as a winner or a loser.

Avoidable problems

From earlier chapters in this book you will have noted where mistakes can arise in your marathon preparation. The first and most obvious is that you are not ready to run the distance simply because you have not done enough or the right kind of training. Even if you've done the right training, you may pay the price for not paying sufficient attention to your diet or to the importance of refuelling and rehydrating during and after training and in the course of your marathon. The use of poor or inappropriate footwear and running gear might cause you a problem. If you don't give enough thought to your race-day travel arrangements, you might find yourself arriving late for the start of the race. You may simply be found out on race-day because, even though you're at a peak of physical fitness, you fail to approach the event with sufficient caution and respect for running at a level pace. Look back to some of the earlier chapters if you are still unclear about how to avoid these all too common mistakes.

Sometimes it's only by making mistakes that you more fully understand the importance of getting things right. So, if you have a disappointing race performance, be prepared to learn from your experience and make amends in your next race. Analyse what went wrong (e.g. were you unable to reach your peak at the right time? Or was your pace judgement at fault? Or did you not devote sufficient attention to your mental preparation?) and take action. Often it helps to discuss these matters with a coach, and where necessary with a sports psychologist.

Unpredictable problems

Despite all your best efforts, you may find that you succumb to illness or injury in the days leading up to the race. Even the world's best marathon runners are not immune to such misfortune: Liz McColgan suffered an insect bite to her foot just days before the Atlanta Olympic Marathon. You may be unlucky in the race itself: Hiromi Taniguchi, the 1991 World Marathon Champion, was tripped at a drinks station midway through the Barcelona Olympic Marathon. The list of potential hazards waiting to ensnare you – from a twisted ankle to a dog bite, from food poisoning to the common cold – is enough to make you feel at least a little 'on edge' as you approach the day of your marathon.

How should you react if you are unlucky enough to confront such adversity? Sometimes, the illness or injury leaves you with no other option than to withdraw from the race. You should then ensure that you have fully recovered before committing yourself to another race. If you're in any doubt about the state of your recovery, give yourself time to do at least one good training session before deciding on your next race.

Often, it is harder to decide whether or not you should pull out from your intended marathon. You appear to be over the worst of your injury or illness, but you have not had time to test yourself in training as you have eased down for competition. Withdrawing from the race would represent a huge disappointment. Not only would you be missing the race that for so long has been the focus of your training; you might also feel that you were letting down all your friends who are

Refusing to give in: despite an insect bite to her foot, Liz McColgan finishes 16th in the 1996 Olympic Marathon

supporting you for charity. On the other hand, by starting the race you would run the risk of performing well below your expectations – or even of not finishing – with little room for a second chance. With the marathon, caution should be your guide. In the long run, you may be doing more harm to your health and your confidence by taking risks. If in doubt, seek counsel from a coach or friend who, while understanding your motivation, can offer a more dispassionate opinion.

Remember too that if you do decide to withdraw from a marathon, there are plenty of other races keen to have your entry. Unlike the London Marathon, many of these can be entered on the day.

Whichever way you decide, your race performance will in part be determined by how well you can put misfortune behind you. In other words, focus on what you can still achieve – even if you have to revise your goals – rather than on what you might have achieved had things turned out differently. In McColgan's case, where the next Olympic opportunity was four years away, she had little option other than to start the race in Atlanta: her 16th place finish, while a personal disappointment, demonstrated her fortitude in overcoming adversity.

Your ability to deal with the unexpected – for instance, a last-minute change in the weather, in the route of the marathon or in race-day arrangements – will depend on your state of mental preparation. You should make contingency plans where you can foresee possible problems. You should also rehearse that feeling of staying calm and unperturbed by these external events. *Your* performance is the one thing over which you can have the most influence, so it is vital that you stay focused on this task as the race approaches.

Moving on

What happens once your marathon has been run?

Your first priority should be to restore your life to a semblance of normality again. Having let your training and thoughts about running your marathon occupy many of your waking moments over the past few weeks, you (and no doubt other members of your family) will benefit from switching off from running for a while and devoting more time to those things that were neglected during your marathon preparation.

When the highs and lows of race-day have worn off, you will be in a better frame of mind to consider the 'Never again!' you uttered as you crossed the finish line at the end of your marathon. It would *not* be unnatural, having done all that training, for you soon to rediscover the urge to lace up your running shoes once more . . .

There is something about running that draws us back for more. Whatever our age or experience, running provides us with new challenges. Despite the saying that 'you're only as good as your last race', many runners are more interested in their *next* one. I hope that the same is true for you.

Reflecting on the disappointment of finishing 4th at the 1994 European Championship Marathon in Helsinki

My wife Gail makes up for the disappointment of being forced to withdraw through illness from the 1999 London Marathon by finishing 2nd in the Stratford Marathon one week later.

Key points

Learn from your mistakes.

Resist the temptation to run your marathon if you are still suffering the effects of illness or injury.

Be prepared to revise your goals if your plans change, and focus on what is ahead.

Give yourself a good recovery period after your marathon.

Learning from my mistakes

Shortly after running the 1997 London Marathon, I had to decide whether or not to accept my place to run for Britain in the 1997 World Championship Marathon in Athens. I wanted to compete for Britain in another championship race, but I was unsure whether I was ready to put myself through another three months of gruelling marathon training so soon after my last period of marathon preparation.

In the end I decided to accept my place to run in Athens. I am always motivated to train hard for championship races. There was the added attraction of running over the ancient course from Marathon to Athens. I also felt that I might not need to train quite as hard or for quite as long as I had for the London race – since I already had a good bank of fitness from earlier in the year.

The build-up

Three weeks after the London Marathon I was back into training and planning my build-up for the race in Athens. Within a week of starting some hard sessions, I began to experience discomfort in my foot – similar to when I was injured in 1995, only now the problem was in my other foot. Once again, I was reduced to doing much of my training in the pool and on the exercise bike.

As the pain abated, I went back to see the specialist who had advised me about my previous foot injury, and was relieved to be told that the problem had eased sufficiently for me to resume normal training. There were now 7½ weeks remaining until the marathon – just enough time, I felt, for me to return to peak fitness. Ahead of me was a three-week stint back at Font Romeu, where I hoped to complete the hardest phase of training before the marathon in Athens.

Going for broke

Over those next three weeks I trained harder than ever before. Assisted by Keith Anderson, who on the eve of his 40th birthday proved to be one of my most enthusiastic training partners, I made the mistake of trying to extend the limits of my training. Once we were over our initial five-day period of acclimatisation, we followed a five-day cycle of training that included a long run of 35–40 km, a tempo run of 20–25 km, and a 10 km workout – plus two days in which we sometimes went beyond our stated intention of running at a steady pace. Over the course of the next 15 days we completed this cycle three times, which meant running 10 hard workouts in the space of just over two weeks. Over the entire 21-day period of our stay, we ran over 400 miles.

We were relieved to get to the end of our stay at altitude still in one piece. We had survived without succumbing to injury or illness, and without breaking down with exhaustion – or so we thought.

On my return home I had an easy week of training, reducing the volume from around 140 miles per week to just over 100. With two weeks to go, I did my last really hard session before the race. I still felt tired while doing this session, but I knew there were a further two weeks of tapering before the day of the marathon.

A flat battery

With 12 days to go, I went out to a training camp in Italy, to acclimatise to the Mediterranean heat that we would have to endure in Athens. I continued to reduce my training, in the hope that I would soon start to get some bounce back into my legs as the race drew nearer.

What I actually experienced, however, was quite the opposite. Even going out for a short run felt like really hard work. My body seemed to be slowly grinding to a halt. I was still eating and sleeping normally, and wasn't feeling ill. It was just that I couldn't run. Whenever I tried to put one foot in front of the other and break out into a jog, I couldn't keep going for more than a few hundred metres – as if my body were failing to respond to its usual operating signals. Painfully, I was being made to realise that I would have to withdraw from the marathon in Athens.

Learning the lessons

I had made the mistake of trying to play 'catch-up' with my original training schedule, which had been interrupted by another foot injury. My frustration at this setback had increased my determination to regain peak fitness, as a consequence of which I had taken too big a risk while training at altitude. I had crammed in too many hard sessions and not given myself sufficient recovery periods – especially important at altitude, where you need longer to recover after intense workouts. At the start of my preparation for Athens, I had acknowledged that I would not need to repeat the intensity of training that I had achieved for my two previous marathons. But I had strayed from these good intentions and, as a result, overdone my training.

I had learned the simple truth that more is not always better. I had trained harder than ever before in the run-up to the 1996 Olympic Marathon, and it had paid off. The same had again been true of my preparation for the London Marathon the following April.

'I had learned the simple truth that more is not always better.'

But now, in the build-up to Athens, I had overstepped the thin line between being super-fit and being over-trained. Now the training had to stop.

A last-minute offer to help out with the BBC commentary on the marathon in Athens distracted my attention from the obvious disappointment of not being able to take part in the race myself. On my return home, I had a number of blood tests to see if my problem could be more clearly identified, and thereafter took my customary end-of-season break. My recovery period would be longer than usual, however, to give myself every chance of making a full recovery from what I had suffered over the summer. Then it was back to the drawing board – time to plan my next campaign.

Appendices

Richard Nerurkar: career details

Date	Event	Finishing position	Time
Championship marathons			
31 October 1993	World Cup Marathon	1st	2:10:03
14 August 1994	European Championship Marathon	4th	2:11:56
12 August 1995	World Championship Marathon	7th	2:15:47
4 August 1996	Olympic Marathon	5th	2:13:39
22 August 1998	European Championship Marathon	8th	2:14:02
City marathons			
23 May 1993	Hamburg Marathon	1st	2:10:57
19 March 1995	Kyongju Marathon	2nd	2:11:03
13 April 1997	London Marathon	5th	2:08:36
Track championships			
27 August 1990	European Championship 10,000 m	5th	28:07
26 August 1991	World Championship 10,000 m	5th	27:57
3 August 1992	Olympic 10,000 m	17th	28:48
Cross-country championships			
19 March 1989	World Cross-country Championships	49th	
24 March 1990	World Cross-country Championships	18th	
24 March 1991	World Cross-country Championships	52nd	
21 March 1992	World Cross-country Championships	15th	
11 December 1994	European Cross-country Championships	25th	
Best times: track			
15 July 1992	3000 m – IAAF Nice Grand Prix	9th	7:48:00
10 August 1990	5000 m – IAAF Brussels Grand Prix	5th	13:23:31
10 July 1993	10,000 m – IAAF Oslo Grand Prix	4th	27:40:03
Best times: road			
31 July 1994	10 km – BUPA Great Welsh Run	2nd	28:25
17 October 1993	10 M – Twickenham Cabbage Patch	1st	46:02
14 April 1996	½ Mar – Paris Humarathon	4th	61:06

Training for the half-marathon

The table below should help you plan out your own half-marathon training programme according to your level of fitness and time goals. The ideal length of time for your build-up is 12 weeks, comprising 10 weeks of good training followed by a two-week taper. You should aim to run at least one race (e.g. 10 km or 10 M) midway through your build-up.

Level	Time goal (hours)	Sessions per week	Miles per week	Weekly long run* (miles)	Quality sessions**
Beginner***	1:50–2:20	4–5	15–25	5–8 (10)	Fartlek + tempo run
Regular runner	1:30–1:50	5–6	30–40	8–11 (13)	Repetitions + tempo runs
Advanced	Faster than 1:30	6–7	40–50	12–14 (15)	Repetitions + tempo runs

*On a regular basis (longest)
**In addition to easy/steady running and long run
***This follows on from the programme for beginners in Chapter 1

Over the course of your build-up you should aim to increase the volume of some of your quality sessions. A beginner, for example, might start with a total of 10–12 minutes of fast running (2 x 5 min or 3 x 4 min) and aim to build up to 20+ minutes (3 x 7 min or 4 x 6 min). The key sessions for the half-marathon, in addition to your long run, are the repetition workouts where you are running for an interval of 4–10 minutes at close to your 10 km racing speed. You can vary your sessions of faster running by changing the length of interval. For a change from interval running, you might decide to do some hills, a pyramid session (e.g. 2 sets of 1 min-2 min-3 min-2 min-1 min) or some fartlek.

A sample week's training halfway through the build-up might look something like this:

Day	Beginner	Regular	Advanced
Monday	30 min easy	35 min easy	35 min easy
Tuesday	35 min inc. 5 x 1 min + 5 x 30s fast	6 x 3 min fast, 2 min recovery	6 x 1 km, 2 min recovery
Wednesday	Rest	30 min easy	45 min easy
Thursday	3 x 5 min fast, 2 min recovery	10 min + 5 min + 5 min fast, 3 min recovery	6–7 M fartlek
Friday	Rest	Rest	Rest
Saturday	35 min easy	30 min easy	3 x 2 M, 3 min recovery
Sunday	7 M long run	10 M long run	13 M long run
Total	22–24 M	34–36 M	45–47 M

Your two-week taper for the half-marathon should follow a similar pattern to your marathon training: training volume is reduced and sessions of faster running are designed to get you used to running at your intended race-pace.

Marathon training programmes

(a)   For sub 5:00 marathon
(b)   For sub 4:00 marathon
(c)   For sub 3:30 marathon
(d)   For sub 2:45 marathon
(e)   For sub 2:20 marathon

Key

M = miles
km = kilometres
m = metres
min = minutes

s = seconds
hr = hour(s)
, 2 min = with 2 minutes recovery
* = @ marathon pace

Note: All weekly totals are given in miles.

(a) Programme for sub 5:00 marathon

Week	Monday	Tuesday	Wednesday
Week 1	Rest	20–25 min easy	Rest
Week 2	Rest	6 x 200 m hills	20–25 min easy
Week 3	Rest	6 x 2 min fast, 2 min jog/walk	20–25 min easy
Week 4	Rest	8 x 1 min fast, 2 min	4 M easy
Week 5	Rest	3 x 1 km, 4 min	3 M easy
Week 6	Rest	4 M easy	4 M easy
Week 7	Rest	6 x 3 min fast, 2 min	3 M easy
Week 8	Rest	3 x 8 min, 3 min	4 M easy
Week 9	Rest	3 M easy	5 M easy
Week 10	Rest	4 x 1 km, 3 min	Rest
Week 11	Rest	3 x 10 min*, 3 min	Rest
Week 12	Rest	2 x 1 M*, 3 min	Rest

Note: For sessions of faster running, run 1 M (8–10 min) easy warm-up/warm-down

(b) Programme for sub 4:00 marathon

Week	Monday	Tuesday	Wednesday
Week 1	Rest	40 min easy	Rest
Week 2	Rest	10 x 1 min, 2 min	4 M easy
Week 3	Rest	8 x 150 m hills	4 M easy
Week 4	Rest	8 x 2 min, 2 min	5 M easy
Week 5	Rest	4 x 1 km, 3 min	4 M easy
Week 6	Rest	6 M easy	5 M steady
Week 7	Rest	6 x 3 min, 2 min	4 M easy
Week 8	Rest	15 + 10 + 5 min fast, 3 min	4 M easy
Week 9	Rest	5 M easy	8 x 1 min, 1 min + 8 x 30 s, 30 s
Week 10	Rest	4 M easy	5 M steady
Week 11	Rest	3 x 10 min*, 3 min	5 M easy
Week 12	Rest	2 x 1 M*, 3 min	Rest

Note: For sessions of faster running, run 10–12 min warm-up/warm-down

Thursday	Friday	Saturday	Sunday	Total
6 x 1 min fast, 2 min	Rest	30 min steady	1:30 hr walk/jog	18
2 x (1 km fast, 4 min walk)	Rest	35 min steady	1:30 hr walk/jog	22
40 min steady	Rest	25 min fartlek	1:45 hr	25
Timed run over 3 M	Rest	4 M steady	1:45 hr	28
3 M easy + strides	Rest	Rest	10 km race	18
8 x 150 m hills	Rest	5 M steady	2 hr	28
Timed run over 5 M	Rest	10 x 1 min/1 min fartlek	2:20 hr	30
8 x (90 s, 90 s)	Rest	4 M easy or rest	½ Mar race or 2:40 hr	35
10 + 6 + 3 min fast, 3 min	Rest	4 M easy	3 hr	35
Timed run over 6 M	Rest	4 M easy	1:30 hr	25
4 M easy + strides	Rest	10 x 1 min/1 min fartlek	1 hr	20
20 min easy	Rest	15 min easy or rest	Marathon	10 + race

Thursday	Friday	Saturday	Sunday	Total
3 x 1 M, 3 min	Rest	4 M easy	1:15 hr	22
4 x 1 km, 3 min	Rest	4 M easy	1:30 hr	26
Timed run over 4 M	Rest	4 M easy	1:45 hr	30
1-2-3-4-3-2-1 min pyramid	Rest	5 M easy	2 hr	36
4 M easy + strides	Rest	Rest	10 km/10 M race	25
3 x 8 min, 3 min	Rest	8 x 200 m hills	2:15 hr	36
Timed run over 6 M	Rest	7 M steady	2:30 hr	40
4 M easy + strides	Rest	Rest	½ Mar race	35
8 M easy	Rest	7 M steady	3 hr	46
2 x 20 min*, 5 min	Rest	6 M steady	1:30 hr	35
Rest	Rest	Rest	1 hr	25
3 M easy	Rest	2 M easy or rest	Marathon	10 + race

(c) Programme for sub 3:30 marathon

Week	Monday	Tuesday	Wednesday
Week 1	5 M easy	5 x 3 min, 2 min	5 M easy
Week 2	5 M easy	10 x 45 s hills	5 M easy
Week 3	5 M easy	2 x (2 km + 1 km), 3 min	5 M easy
Week 4	Rest	8 x 2 min, 2 min	5 M easy
Week 5	Rest	6 M easy	a.m. 4 M easy p.m. 12 x 1 min, 1 min
Week 6	5 M easy	a.m. 4 M easy p.m. 5 x 1 km	5 M easy
Week 7	5 M easy	a.m. 4 M easy p.m. 10 x 2 min, 2 min	5 M easy
Week 8	5 M easy	a.m. 3 M easy p.m. 3 x 1 M, 3 min	6 M easy
Week 9	Rest	6 M easy	a.m. 5 M easy p.m. 6 x 1 km, 3 min
Week 10	Rest	5 M easy	a.m. 3 M easy p.m. 6 M steady
Week 11	4 M easy	6 M brisk	5 M easy
Week 12	3 M easy	2 x 1 M*, 2 min	Rest

Thursday	Friday	Saturday	Sunday	Total
5–6 M fartlek	Rest	6 M steady	12 M	40
Timed run over 4 M	Rest	6 M steady	14 M	45
5–6 M fartlek	Rest	8 x 1 min hills	16 M	50
5 M easy + strides	Rest	3 M easy	10 km/10 M race	30
5 M easy	1 x 2 M, 4 min + 2 x 1 M, 3 min	6 M steady	16 M	50
a.m. 4 M easy p.m. 5–6 M fartlek	Rest	Timed run over 5 M	18 M	55
3 x 2 km, 3 min	Rest	8 M steady	20 M	55
5 M easy + strides	Rest or 4 M easy	Rest	½ Mar race	40–45
5 M easy	a.m. 5 M easy p.m. 6 M brisk	4 M easy	22 M	60
3 x 10 min, 3 min	5 M easy	10 x 400 m, 90 s	14 M	45
6 M steady + strides	Rest	3 km + 2 km + 1 km*, 3 min	8 M	35
3 M easy	Rest	2 M easy or rest	Marathon	15 + race

(d) Programme for sub 2:45 marathon

Week	Monday	Tuesday	Wednesday
Week 1	a.m. 5 M easy p.m. 5 M steady	6 x 3 min, 2 min	a.m. 5 M easy p.m. 5 M steady
Week 2	a.m. 5 M easy p.m. 5 M steady	8 x 150 m hills	a.m. 5 M easy p.m. 5 M steady
Week 3	a.m. 5 M easy p.m. 5 M steady	4 x 1 M, 2 min	a.m. 5 M easy p.m. 5 M steady
Week 4	a.m. 5 M easy p.m. 5 M steady	10 x 2 min, 2 min	a.m. 5 M easy p.m. 5 M steady
Week 5	a.m. 5 M easy p.m. 5 M steady	8 x 150 m hills	a.m. 5 M easy p.m. 5 M steady
Week 6	5 M easy	6 M fartlek	a.m. 5 M easy p.m. 5 M steady
Week 7	a.m. 5 M easy p.m. 5 M steady	1-2-3-4-3-2-1 min pyramid	a.m. 5 M easy p.m. 5 M steady
Week 8	a.m. 5 M easy p.m. 5 M steady	2 x 1 M, 2 min + 2 x 1/2 M, 90 s + 4 x 400 m, 1 min	5 M easy
Week 9	5 M easy	6 M steady or easy fartlek	a.m. 5 M easy p.m. 5 M steady
Week 10	5 M easy	a.m. 4 M easy p.m. 7 M brisk	5 M easy + strides
Week 11	6 M easy	6 M fartlek	5 M easy
Week 12	5 M easy	2 x 1 M*, 2 min	Rest

Thursday	Friday	Saturday	Sunday	Total
5 M fartlek	4 M easy or rest	5 M steady	14 M	50
Tempo run over 5 M	5 M easy	5 M steady	16 M	55
6 x 250 m hills	5 M easy	2 M easy + strides	10 km/10 M race	50
3 x 2 km, 3 min	a.m. 5 M easy p.m. 5 M steady	5 M steady	18 M	60
6 M easy + strides	Rest	2–3 M easy	10 M–20 M race	50–60
8 x 1 km, 3 min	a.m. 5 M easy p.m. 6 M steady	Timed run over 8 M	20 M	65
4 x 2 km, 3 min	a.m. 5 M easy p.m. 6 M steady	5 M steady	22 M	70+
5 M easy + strides	Rest	2–3 M easy	½ Mar race	45
3 x 3 km, 3 min	a.m. 5 M easy p.m. 5 M steady	8 x 2 min, 2 min	24 M	75
2 x 5 km*, 4 min	5 M easy	6 M steady	15M	55
8 M brisk	Rest	5 M steady + strides	10 M	40
3 M easy + strides	Rest	2 M easy or rest	Marathon	15 + race

(e) Programme for sub 2:20 marathon

Week	Monday	Tuesday	Wednesday
Week 1	a.m. 6 M easy p.m. 6 M steady	a.m. 4 M easy p.m. 4 x 1 M, 2 min	12 M easy
Week 2	a.m. 6 M easy p.m. 6 M steady	a.m. 4 M easy p.m. 3 x 3 km, 3 min	12 M easy
Week 3	a.m. 6 M easy p.m. 6 M steady	a.m. 5 M easy p.m. 8 x 1 km, 90 s	13 M easy
Week 4	a.m. 6 M easy p.m. 6 M steady	a.m. 5 M easy p.m. 4 x (1600 m + 400 m), 1 min/2 min	13 M easy
Week 5	a.m. 6 M easy p.m. 6 M steady	16 M easy	a.m. 6 M easy p.m. 10 M steady
Week 6	a.m. 6 M easy p.m. 10 M steady	a.m. 6 M easy p.m. 6 x 1 M, 2 min	14 M easy
Week 7	Rest	5 M easy	8 M easy
Week 8	a.m. 6 M easy p.m. 6 M steady	5 x 2 km @ mar pace, 1 km @ 30 s slower	14 M easy
Week 9	a.m. 6 M easy p.m. 6 M steady	a.m. 6 M easy p.m. 2 x 2 M, 2 min + 2 x 1 M, 90 s	14 M easy
Week 10	Rest	a.m. 5 M easy p.m. 6 M steady	10 M easy
Week 11	Rest	a.m. 4 M easy p.m. 2 x 6 km @ mar pace, 4 min	a.m. 5 M easy p.m. 5 M steady
Week 12	5 M easy	8–10 M steady finishing briskly	Rest

*First 5 M easy, next 10 M steady, last 5 M @ mar pace

Thursday	Friday	Saturday	Sunday	Total
a.m. 6 M easy p.m. 8 M steady	6 M easy	8 M inc. 20 min fartlek	16 M	80
a.m. 6 M easy p.m. 8 M steady + strides	a.m. 4 M easy p.m. 6 x 800 m, 2 min	Rest	18 M	80
a.m. 5 M easy p.m. 6–7 M fartlek	8 M steady	40 min tempo run	18–20 M	90
a.m. 5 M easy p.m. 5 M easy + strides	Rest	4 M easy	10 km race	65
a.m. 5 M easy p.m. 4 x 2 km @ mar pace, 1 km @ 30 s slower	Rest	a.m. 8 M inc. 20 x 30 s, 30 s p.m. 4 M easy	20 M	90
a.m. 5 M easy p.m. 8 M steady + strides	a.m. 5 M easy p.m. 5 M steady	4 M easy	½ Mar race	90
a.m. 5 M easy p.m. 5 M easy	10 M steady	8 M inc. 20 min fartlek	22–24 M	70
a.m. 6 M easy p.m. 6 M steady	a.m. 5 M easy p.m. 10 x 2 min, 90 s	10 M easy	24 M	95
a.m. 6 M easy p.m. 10 M steady	a.m. 5 M easy p.m. 5 M steady	8 M inc. 20 x 30 s, 30 s	20 M tempo run*	100
10 M easy	a.m. 5 M easy p.m. 6 M steady	a.m. 2 x (8 x 400 m, 45 s), 3 min p.m. 5 M easy	14 M	75
6 M easy	a.m. 7 M inc. 20 x 30 s, 30 s p.m. 5 M easy	Rest	12 M	55
4 M easy + strides	Rest	2–3 M easy	Marathon	20 + race

Stretching for marathon runners

Stretching is discussed in Chapter 1, p. 16, in the context of the warm-up and warm-down. It is important, because it can help you to stay injury-free; it keeps your muscles loose and reduces or prevents post-exercise stiffness.

As a general rule, stretching should be performed both pre- and post-exercise, with your warm-up stretches carried out after a brief jog – it's best to stretch when your muscles are already warm. You should be able to feel the muscle extending, but not to a point at which it becomes painful. If it hurts, decrease the stretch – or stop it altogether. Hold the stretch for 15–20 seconds; don't bounce but keep it steady.

The following is a routine of five or six simple stretches which I do at the end of each training run. For more detailed advice refer to any established book on the subject, such as *The Complete Guide to Stretching* by Christopher M. Norris (A & C Black).

Calves

Lengthens and stretches the gastrocnemius and soleus muscles at the back of the lower leg.

Starting position

Stand facing a wall or post, in a 'half-lunge' position with your right foot forwards. Your feet should be parallel and about hip-width apart. Place your hands on the wall.

The stretch (gastrocnemius)

Push against the wall/post with your right (front) leg bent, and your back leg extended with the knee locked. Keep the heel of your back leg firmly on the ground throughout the stretch. Repeat on the other side. (This stretch can also be executed with both feet together as illustrated.)

The stretch (soleus)

As above, but bend your back knee slightly to alter the emphasis of the stretch to the lower calf.

Gastrocnemius stretch

Soleus stretch

Quadriceps (front of thighs)

Lengthens and stretches the quadriceps muscles at the front of the thigh. If the hips are tilted forwards, this will also stretch the hip flexors (*see* below).

Starting position and stretch

Standing on your left leg – using a wall or training partner for balance, if necessary – flex your right leg and grip the ankle with your right hand. Pull your heel towards the centre of your right buttock cheek and hold (you can use your hand to increase the range of motion). Repeat on the other side. Throughout the stretch, ensure that your hips are facing forwards and avoid hollowing your lower back.

Adductors (inner thighs)

Lengthens and stretches the adductor muscles, on the inside of the thigh.

Starting position and stretch

Sit on the ground with your back upright – if necessary, against a wall. Place the soles of your feet together and let your knees lower gently towards the floor, until you obtain a comfortable stretch inside the thigh and groin. Your hands can either be placed on the floor behind your back, to help keep the spine in an upright position, or used to press on the inside of your knees to increase the stretch. (An alternative to this stretch is to straddle your legs out wide and straight, easing your legs apart with your hands by applying pressure on the inside of your knees.)

Quadriceps stretch

Adductors stretch

Hamstrings (back of thighs)

Lengthens and stretches the hamstring muscles at the back of the thigh.

Starting position and stretch

Sit upright on the floor with your right leg extended – but not fully 'locked' at the knee – in front of you. Your left leg should be bent and angled slightly out to the side, with the knee facing out. Bend forwards from the hips until you feel a stretch in the back of the right thigh. Don't hunch your back; keep your chin up as you lean gently forwards. Repeat on the other side. You can also do this exercise standing, with one leg resting on a bench at knee height.

Gluteals (buttocks)

Lengthens and stretches the gluteal muscles in the buttocks.

Starting position and stretch

Either lie on the floor with your left leg straight (as illustrated), or sit on the floor with your back upright and your left leg extended out in front of you. Bend your right leg and cross it over your left, with your foot as close in to your body as is comfortably possible. Wrapping your left arm around your right leg as shown, 'hug' the knee into your body until you feel a stretch in your right buttock. Hold, then repeat on the other side.

Hamstrings stretch

Gluteals stretch

Iliopsoas (hip flexors)

Lengthens and stretches the iliopsoas muscle, running through to the front of the femur (thigh bone) from the pelvis and lumbar spine.

Starting position and stretch

Kneel on the floor. Step your right leg forwards into a lunge position, with the foot flat on the floor. Keep the knee of your left leg on the floor. Press the hips forwards until you feel a stretch. You can rest your hands on your hips, on your right knee, or on the floor to help you keep your balance. Keep your chest 'lifted' and your back straight. Repeat on the other side.

Iliopsoas stretch

Weights and circuits for marathon runners

As with the stretches on pp. 156–160 it is beyond the scope of this book to provide anything more than general guidelines on weights and circuits. For more specific information and illustrations of the exercises, refer to an established book, like Anita Bean's *Complete Guide to Strength Training* (A & C Black).

How much and how often? In general, the more time and energy you devote to your running training, the less you can give to alternative forms of training. This means that the best time to do this form of training is during a period of relatively little running. Three short (20-minute) sessions per week is better than a once-weekly hour-long session; do half this amount for 'maintenance' during a period of harder running training.

Main objectives: all-round body conditioning, addressing in particular any muscle weaknesses and thus reducing the likelihood of injury.

Weights or circuits? Do what you enjoy most and what comes more easily – circuits, for instance, though more enjoyable when done with a group in the gym, can be done in your living room at the end of a run. The key thing is to focus on your own weaknesses in core muscles (*see* tables below).

General guidelines for using weights

- Use weight machines, rather than free weights, to isolate key muscle groups.
- Seek advice from a gym instructor about operation of machines.
- To guard against overstrain, do more repetitions with lighter weights.
- Aim to maintain a smooth, steady rhythm as you lift – don't jerk your effort.

Addressing weaknesses using weights

Part of body	Purpose	Exercises
Quadriceps, gluteals and hamstrings	To maintain strength balance between quadriceps and hamstrings, and protect against overstrain	Leg presses; hamstring curls; quadriceps lifts; squats with bar on shoulder
Back	To improve running posture and prevent weaknesses leading to hip and hamstring problems	Lateral pull-downs; back extensions
Abdominals	To maintain efficient running posture and stabilise trunk	Sit-ups, perhaps even with bean-bag weight on top of stomach
Arms	To maintain good form, especially at end of race	Triceps dips

Addressing weaknesses through circuit training

For a 20-minute session, complete the programme below twice, i.e. 2 x 10 min circuit (8 x 60 sec, 15 sec recovery).

Part of body	Exercise	Description of exercise
Back	Arches	Lie on front with arms in 'hands-up' position; keeping lower body on the floor, raise upper body (from waist up) off floor
Abdominals	Crunches	Lie on back with knees pulled up towards stomach, feet held together off floor and hands behind head; raise head so that elbows touch knees
Hips and gluteals	Side leg raise*	Lie on side, resting only on elbow and side of bottom foot (and knee if necessary). Raise top leg for 10 sec hold, and repeat 4 times
Arms and chest	Press-ups	Do not let back arch by keeping head, neck and spine in straight line
Back and abdominals	Straight leg raise*	Press-up position, but resting on forearms (not hands); keeping back straight and squeezing buttocks together, raise alternate legs off ground for 30 sec hold
Abdominals	Scissors	Lie on back with legs raised slightly off floor – one bent, the other extended – with one arm extended forwards towards knee, the other back behind head; alternately move forwards and back opposite arm and leg
Hips and hamstrings	Straight leg extension*	Lie on back with knees bent and feet on floor. Raise hips off ground, keeping weight on head, shoulders and arms, hips held high and buttocks squeezed. Alternately extend one leg towards ceiling for 30 sec hold
Arms	Running arms	Standing with one foot forwards, shoulders relaxed and elbow fixed at 90°, adopt fast running-arm action

*In contrast to the other exercises involving fast continuous motion, these exercises strengthen the muscle groups through a process of holding in a stable position.

Useful addresses

UK Athletics
Athletics House
10 Harborne Road
Edgbaston
Birmingham B15 3AA
www.ukathletics.org

London Marathon Ltd
PO Box 1234
London SE1 8RZ
www.london-marathon.co.uk

Runners World
7–10 Chandos Street
London W1M 0AD
www.runnersworld.co.uk

Running Fitness
Emap Active
Apex House
Oundle Road
Peterborough PE2 9NP
www.onrunning.com/runningfitness

**Organisation of Chartered
Physiotherapists in Private Practice**
Cedar House
Bell Plantation
Watling Street
Towcester
North Hants NN12 6HN
www.physiofirst.org.uk

London School of Sports Massage
(with nationwide directory)
28 Station Parade
Willesden Green
London NW2 4NX
www.massage-therapy.demon.co.uk

Leisure Pursuits Group
(sports tour operators)
Essex House
Essex Road
Basingstoke
Hampshire RG21 8SU
www.leisurepursuits.com

Sports Tours International
91 Walkden Road
Walkden
Manchester M28 5DQ
Tel.: 0161-703 8161

Index

rtin, Eamonn 23, 90, 127
medical screen 94
menstrual cycle 19
mental preparation 72–3
Moneghetti, Steve 79, 89–92, 130
monitoring condition 41, 46, 93–4
motivation 1–3, 28–9, 46, 105, 107, 109, 131

negative splits 115
Nyahururu 133–4

Olympics
    Atlanta, *see* marathon races
    Barcelona 84–6, 136
    trials 93
overtraining 14, 112, 141

pace-makers 116–18
peak performance 44, 81
periodisation 105–11
Perszke, Wieslaw 123
Peters, Jim 115
physiotherapy, *see* rehabilitation
Pilkington, Paul 117
Pinto, Antonio 89–92, 119
Pippig, Uta 48, 130
Plaatjes, Mark 119–20
psychologist 94, 136
Punkalaidun 64

race
    your first 16–17
racing
    'back-to-front' 115
    experience 81–7
    financial bonuses 116
    gun-to-tape 115
    strategies 73–4
    unpredictable elements 136–8
recharging batteries 107
recovery 58–60, 69–71, 139
    measures for post-race 61–3
rehabilitation 97–9
    ice foot-baths 98
    physiotherapy 94–5, 99
rest 19, 46, 58–60, 71, 96, 98, 107
resting pulse 93
running gear, *see* clothing

running magazines 19, 110, 132
running shoes, *see* clothing

safety 17
Shorter, Frank 115
Smith, Geoff 20
support services 94–5, 125–6

Taniguchi, Hiromi 136
Thugwane, Josiah 44, 79, 81, 89–92
time-trial 83
training
    alternative forms of 60, 109, 111
    break from 29, 111
    consistency 41
    devising routes 45
    fartlek 41
    graduated approach 9, 25–6, 99
    intensity 25, 27, 37, 40, 42, 71
    long run 37, 39–40
    partner 9, 17, 60, 125
    progression 25–6, 42
    repetitions 40, 42
    routine 9, 38–9, 53
    strides 15, 41
    tempo run 41–3
    timing 11
variety 14, 107
    volume 25–6, 42, 72
    warm-down 10, 96
    warm-up 10, 96
training camp life 126–31
    Algarve 126, 132
    at altitude 32, 128
    Boulder 48–9
    Font Romeu 34, 64, 129–30, 140
    Kenya 70, 128–9, 133–4
    Lanzarote 127, 132
    Solvalla 64–5
    Tallahassee 77–8
    Tirrenia 51, 92
    warm-weather 128, 133
Tulloh, Bruce and Sue 21–3, 30–1, 33, 40, 46,
    64–5, 77, 86, 122–4

Vergouwen, Peter 101

winning 3–4
Woking 10-Mile 46–7, 52